COMMONSENSE WISDOM LEADERSHIP

Organizations are from Mars - Employees are from Venus

STEPHEN HISS

ISBN
978-1-963254-23-5 (Paperback)
978-1-963254-24-2 (eBook)
978-1-963254-22-8 (Hardcover)

TABLE OF CONTENTS

ACKNOWLEDGMENTS

Illustrations are provided by Chamisa Kellogg Kimberly Hiss for providing valuable editing advice David Fogg; Fogg Management Consulting, for taking personal interest in this project and providing advice and encouragement Theresa and Timothy Merkel for their friendship and the suggestions they graciously gave to strengthen this writing

FORWARD

Leadership in the simplest terms can be defined as the art of applying management principals and techniques to everyday workplace situations in order to accomplish a defined outcome. When those two elements [management principals and techniques] are properly applied intelligently with commonsense and wisdom leaders can expect the best possible outcome. That sounds easy enough. Until one other element– people– are added to the mix because that's when management can get complicated in a hurry. The central question is why? I believe it's because knowing management principles is something very different from knowing how those principles can be applied.

While reading Aesop's Fables to my two daughters years ago, I began to appreciate the essential lessons they taught about human nature and began to realize the expectations that are deeply embedded in our human nature. Later, I became aware of how a basic understanding of those expectations can be used to provide strong and effective leadership.

Over the years I have observed competent and experienced managers become frustrated to the point of distraction with workplace problems especially when the time line for taking action is the priority. But these are exactly the times when it is most important to take a breath and realize it is often not the employee [s] per se that we need to manage it is actually those expectations that are embedded in all of our human nature.

So, what is it about adding people [employees] to the workplace that makes managing more complicated? What is the root cause of this complication? Or conversely, what can leaders do to build a stable, productive, and reasonably happy workplace environment?

One of the tools I have used to help explain that illusive element of management are Aesop's fables. For this writing I selected 10 fables because; One, they can be applied directly to a wide range of management situations. Two, they provide a clear window for seeing and understanding employees expectations. Three, such an understanding can provide sound guidelines for how employees can be managed fairly and effectively. And four, they are fun to read and think about so it's more likely we will remember their lessons in times of stress.

Here are a few examples of what I'm talking about. Imbedded in each of us is a need to exercise a measure of independence. We also have a need to exercise our creativity and be appreciated for our efforts. And, along with other deeply embedded human nature expectations, we need to feel safe and have our position in the workplace [and in life] not threatened. These expectations apply directly to management situations because it is the degree to which these expectations are satisfied or are triggered that determines how our employees will act or react.

Here's the rub, coincidentally and necessarily so, organizations have a "nature" of their own. Examples of an organization's nature include things like the need to establish and enforce rules they have [unilaterally] created. Organizations put limits on self-expression and often become weary when employees exercise their own creativity or individuality. Overall, organizations have a legitimate need to control– and so the complexity in management comes when the organization's expectations "push" against the strongest expectations of our human nature, and that is exactly when managers' understanding of these expectations becomes most important. Recognizing this potential conflict [of will] in the workplace helps us answer the central question of why adding people cause management complications. It's actually quite simple to but no less difficult to achieve. It is that managers should avoid focusing on the person[s] or personalities and instead take a more objective approach and find a way to navigate both sets of [expectations]. As I said, this is not always easy to achieve, yet many successful leaders have mastered it. The ten fables, case studies, and discussions that are presented in this text provide simple yet power perspectives and techniques managers can use to mitigate the effect of these competing expectations.

Perhaps this all can be considered in a slightly different and possibly more fun way. Organizations are from Mars– employees are from Venus and the workplace is their playground which managers have to navigate for everyone's benefit.

CHAPTER ONE

TEAM BUILDING

The Oxen and the Lion

A Lion used to prowl about a field in which Four Oxen used to dwell. Many a time he tried to attack them; but whenever he came near they turned their tails to one another, so that whichever way he approached them he was met by the horns of one of them. At last, however, they fell a-quarrelling among themselves, and each went off to pasture alone in a separate corner of the field. Then the Lion attacked them one by one and soon made an end of all four.

United we stand; divided we fall.

Practical Application

A management team will stay strong and unified when its leader appreciates the strengths and weaknesses among its members, works to build competencies, reinforces confidence and trust, provides a clear vision of purpose and process for its members while establishing clear benchmarks for performance.

Case Study

Dave began his new responsibilities as division director of a large healthcare facility and quickly began to see much more clearly the extent and scope of operations problems that had been described during the interview process. He learned his department managers have been working hard to control a wide range of personnel and operations issues but have been largely unsuccessful. They were upset and discouraged because many, if not most, of their efforts to address personnel issues ended in frustration. When a manager asked an employee to perform a task, they felt free to ask the manager why wasn't someone else asked. If an employee made an error that a manager felt needed to be addressed the employee would point to the mistakes others made and would ask, why am I being "picked on." When a manager attempted a formal counseling with HR sitting in, it would most often fail because the HR representative would find flaws in the manager's process or with the documentation. In still other situations, a union representative would sometimes successfully challenge the counseling. The management group felt out maneuvered by employees and threatened by the employee's union. There were other concerns with budget management. Dave had one more serious problem which was the very high vacancy rate his division had been experiencing. It seemed to be virtually impossible to attract candidates to fill vacant positions. In fact, the vacancy rate at one point was between 15 to 20 percent. The only option his managers had was to hire contract labor or temporary employees which was very expensive and did little to build loyalty.

Discussion

After a short time on his new job, it became clear to Dave that his management group was not functioning as a unit, nor did they feel a sense of collegiality that is vital to a high performing group. They also felt ill equipped to manage their "foul-spirited" employees, and blamed their employees for being unwilling to cooperate and help solve problems. Despite these problems, Dave could see that the managers he inherited were intelligent, hardworking, and highly motivated, however, the management techniques they were using were inconsistent and poorly conceived. He saw little evidence of uniformity with management practices, management philosophies, or the techniques they used to address issues. Dave's managers were willing to take action with employees but in many cases the techniques they used were misdirected and too often ended in frustration.

This case study demonstrates what can happen when a central vision of purpose, a well-defined management process, and a clearly stated management philosophy are absent within a management group. They are key elements that can be found with all successful management groups because they function as essential way points for its members to follow and work as a kind of glue which holds everyone together and keeps them moving in the same direction and in the same manner.

Dave learned that his 12 managers were promoted from line positions because they were trusted longtime workers. He also learned they were in their current management positions for an average of five years. And, that none had the benefit of the most basic management training. It was not long before Dave began to suspect the core issue may not be their "mean spirited" employees, but his managers who were poorly equipped to handle the challenges of their current responsibilities. It was clear that the members of his management team had not been properly trained or coached.

Management teams should be able to function in various important ways. They should be their division's support system and brain trust. Its members are responsible for making accurate assessments of their operation which helps their leader make sound decisions. Dave's department managers also need to function as change agents and facilitators for setting performance standards and making operations improvements for their individual departments. And team members also need to gauge and represent their employees to their division director which helps keep him/her to operate in the "real world".

There is a wide range of styles and techniques that successful leaders can use to build and maintain strong and effective management teams, but among all of these are a few important constants. One is to establish a central vision of purpose and of process ["This is how we do things]". These includes having a clear understanding of our primary objective. What is our management philosophy and culture, having a clear understanding of the basic rules, and expectations for performing our management responsibilities. How do we evaluate situations with employees? How do we know when to take action and what is the process for taking action? How much autonomy do department managers have? When a management group leader defines these elements, it creates an environment where everyone can work with greater confidence, are in concert with each other, and can support the organization's vision and objectives.

A management team leader's central responsibility is to create that vision of purpose, process, and philosophy. *The Oxen and the Lion* fable demonstrate what can happen when these vital pieces are missing. It takes a strong and unified team with a clear vision of purpose and process to overcome a myriad of distractions and challenges that are sure to occur in any operation. In the end, management team leaders bring that vision to life with proper coaching, mentoring, and by example.

A Blue Print for Directing Operations

Dave knew his primary job was to have discussions regarding these elements, and to accomplish this, he knew he must create an environment where he can have honest, open, and supportive two-way conversations with his managers during operations meetings and in private. He knew over time these discussions would create a kind of blue print and set of way points his managers could use to establish a higher level of control. When leaders encourage open two-way discussions in a safe environment, it works to build a culture of unity, trust, and group strength even when opinions differ. Working in such an environment also increases managers' confidence as they begin to see how their developing skills and their new vision of purpose and process puts them on a more-firm footing when addressing personnel and operations situations.

Also, as the management team's central vision begins to form their employees will sense a new consistency and uniformity of philosophy and process with their managers which leads them with less opportunity to challenge. This doesn't mean mangers can count on reaching a point of nirvana with their employees where everyone is thrilled with their managers and are eager to cooperate. However, it does mean employee engagement and cooperation is likely to improve because employees will find fewer cracks in management's amour that they can explore. The benefit of this to managers, of course, is their operations are likely to function more smoothly and with less on-the-job stress.

Know When to Lead and When to Follow

Dave knows that he must not become overly confident with his own assessments. Team leaders need to be able to recognize when it's time to stop, listen, and take advice from their managers, and consider alternatives. Being able to sense when to lead and when to follow is an important career survival skill and leadership trait. There are thousands- millions of documented examples in which leaders have described how they were able to avoid serious miss steps or find better solutions by navigating this leadership conundrum.

Leadership strength and control is not measured by being [right] all the time, it is recognized by being smart- all of the time. And that comes from one's ability to see [for a given moment in time] his/her limitations, prejudges, and perspectives may not be the most useful and be open to recommendations from their direct reports- even on occasion from a line employee as we will see later in this writing. I have been in situations where a leader resisted this because they felt doing so would minimize their strength or stature as a leader, but ironically not doing so more often reveals the leader's own insecurities. All this simply means is that a leader's psychological make up needs to be strong enough to allow for and accept other points of view without feeling challenged or minimized.

I have experienced a management team leader's need to dominate conversations to the point where their managers become disengaged and unwilling to use their own problem-solving abilities. The obvious result is that the group's overall performance is minimized. I recall one meeting in particular when several vice presidents were engaged in open, creative, and worthwhile conversation until their bigger than life leader entered the room. At that moment all attention centered around their leader and the discussion was truncated by the effect of his personality. Sometimes we attempt to excuse these bigger than life leaders by pointing to what may appear to be their superior intellect, but as we will see later, superior intellect alone is not an adequate substitute for a lack of leadership character or acumen. Of course, the other side of that approach is when leaders rely too heavily on consensus. This can lead to inconsistencies and ill-advised decision making. It also creates an environment that is unpredictable and leaves managers continually re-calculating how to navigate various situations.

Know the Managers on Your Team

It's important for team leaders to [know] their managers. Before Dave can proceed, he must learn more about his managers. Know what makes them happy and confident with their jobs. Know what excites them and what circumstances makes them feel uncomfortable. What parts of their jobs they enjoy and don't like— and are therefore less likely to perform well? Know what kinds of situations make them feel less confident and even vulnerable, which is when they are more likely to act defensively or possibly too aggressively. This helps leaders to know when to intervene subtly or sometimes more directly and provide support and guidance.

Get to know how each manager views their employees as well. This is helpful because of the way manager's view their employees determines how they are most likely to address situations. Leaders can often make this assessment pretty accurately through simple observations and by sitting in on employee meetings with their manager. Are their meetings problem solving and productive, or are they gab and complaining sessions? Are they conducted in a "business casual" or more formal way with less open discussion. This allows the group leader to better understand, support, and possibly coach his/her managers.

A Manager's Point of View Regarding Employees

I have worked with managers who view their employees as, "they can't be trusted", or "employees are "lazy", or "[they] are only interested in money". With such a perspective, managers are more likely to approach employees in a heavy-handed, arbitrary, and sometimes unreasonable manner and will likely create an unhappy workgroup and a frustrated manager. The opposite can be equally troublesome. If a manager views employees in a too "advisory" way and where decisions are weighted by employee's feelings will often lead to confusion. Dave will have to make these simple but important assessments of his managers.

Dave should also encourage his managers to be aware of themselves. [Know thyself]. What is their management style? Being aware of when their approach to situations works well or not so well can benefit them in many ways and provides an opportunity to make adjustments. There are several simple and easy to use self-assessment tools online that can give perspectives on this. Perhaps having general group discussions about this in these early stages would be helpful. There are, of course, many variations of those two extremes but the point here is when having problems like the one's described above, managers would do well to take a moment to objectively recognize how they view their employees and their approach to various situations. As unnecessary as this may seem, I have worked with managers who were totally unaware of their own leadership style and completely wrong about how they were viewed by their employees

Where Should Dave Start

To this point we uncovered a wide range of very common and troublesome circumstances. Are the personnel problems his managers experience simply because they had too many foul spirited employees, or are Dave's managers the main problem? Where should Dave start. Let's first consider his managers. They were all promoted directly from the "work pool". This case study describes12 intelligent people who were put into challenging situations primarily because they had strong technical skills and a strong work ethic, but without adequate training and coaching they had no choice but to invent their own theories and techniques to solve their personnel and operations situations.

Dave also found the employees were angry and frustrated as well because they were being subjected at times to what could be considered inappropriate and sometimes "crazy" management tactics. And, like the lion in the fable, the employees found ways to take advantage of those "cracks" in management's armor. In the case study, the managers' anger and frustration lead to actions that did little more than provoke their employees even more, which created a continuous circle of passive aggressive employee conduct that in-turn encouraged their managers to create new methods that were just as ineffective. Clearly, all of this feed into their manager's being convinced the basic problem was their employees as they saw themselves working hard to fix problems.

Dave knew several different action plans had to be considered. But first he knew step one is to make a thorough and accurate assessment of the situation overall, and then identify the individual pieces of the puzzle. Dave also needs to know what resources or other support may be available from his boss. Unfortunately, in many cases the reality will be little– the well-intended offers he received from senior management during the interview to help are often short lived. The reality is senior management and Dave's boss hired him to fix the problems and not look for solutions elsewhere– and Dave told them he is their fixer.

All leaders must rely on the wisdom they accumulated from past successes and failures, his time-tested management philosophies, intellect, wisdom, and the commonsense. These are a leader's primary resources, and Dave must apply those resources to fact-find and make accurate assessments before he can think about action plans. He must then use those assessments to create an overall strategy and a set of sufficiently detailed tactics that can lead to implementing his action plans and see the critical path [s] to all of his key operations, personnel, and budget problems.

After making these assessments, Dave saw that a substantial portion of the root cause of the division's personnel management problems was his poorly equipped management team and not the employees. He recognized the [employee problem] was primarily a symptom. The employees certainly were foul spirited, resistant to change for the better, and disruptive, but he also saw why the employees were behaving in that way. He felt sure about this after hearing employees talk at staff meetings and while talking with his managers individually and during their operations meetings. Despite his manager's well intentioned and genuine efforts to resolve problems, he could easily see they were simply not equipped to handle the challenging circumstances they had to deal with, and saw how the employees were able to take full advantage of their managers' mistakes.

He also realized that step 1 is not to accuse, but to begin work on identifying and developing those central vision pieces that his managers can attach themselves to. He must also begin a process of coaching, mentoring, and directing while offering all the support he could provide. The good news is that he could see his managers were smart and had potential, and for the moment, that was all he needed to know. More specific action plans will take hold as his managers gradually use their revised management philosophies, their new vision, and more effective techniques to solve problems.

Department Rounding

One way Dave was able to understand how his managers view their employees was to see what's happening on the floor while rounding through his departments. I tried to make rounds every 30 or 60 days to meet and have casual conversations with employees and their managers. Making general observations of workflow, cleanliness, and getting a sense of employee morale can provide clues about what priorities are given to such things as quality of service, operating efficiencies, and the workplace culture. Employees would talk about their jobs in general terms and sometimes more specifically about the various procedures they perform. They would also say things that told me something about the pride they felt in their work. By having these brief and casual conversations I could see how closely employees are engaged and are able to link their own on-the-job efforts to the organization's mission and objectives.

Sometimes employees would take the opportunity to say hello and talk simply for the purpose of having a brief conversation or might tell me something about what their grandchildren did recently. Other times I would ask about a specific task they perform. In all of these occasions I would be sure to say hello and chat for a few minutes with their manager. These conversations were not weighty in any way and were brief, but they gave employees an opportunity to express themselves in a personal way to management and it gave me an opportunity to learn a little about the nitty gritty of each department's daily activity, or perhaps about a particularly troublesome machine that needs frequent maintenance. All of this also helped me prepare and defend next year's budget.

My hope in rounding was to hear employees express a measure of pride in the work they do. If employes express pride in their work, it indicates to me the operation is healthy. Pride within a work group functions as a kind of essential glue which works to hold employes together as a team with their manager. When I don't get these kinds of comments or sense of enthusiasm it indicates something is missing. Pride within a workgroup strengthens everyone's willingness to work together through difficult situations, and creates an environment that allows managers to reach for continuous improvement with employees who are fully engaged.

Operations Meeting

It is essential for leaders to conduct regularly scheduled operations meetings. These meetings may be with the director and his/her managers or with supervisors and their employees, or even lead people with their coworkers. During operations meeting, directors should talk about their observations. Problems need to be aired and tracked as well. A clearly defined agenda with minutes and updates on previous discussions are important so everyone knows which items were solved, on hold, or otherwise. Successes and failed situations need to get equal attention and there should be clear directions about all the situations that need further attention. As I mentioned earlier, conversations should be collegial but also direct at times when needed. The team leader should always provide for open and respectful two-way conversation especially when opinions differ. Quality of performance issues should always be on the table. The point here is to keep two-way communication going about things that are important to both management and employees.

Keeping the Ball Rolling

It's easy when operations are doing well to feel comfortable. After all everyone worked hard so let's feel good about where we are. But there's a problem if this sense of accomplishment becomes the dominant sentiment because the rest of the world is continually moving forward, and things may be happening that complacency can't anticipate. So, while feeling "good" leaders also need to be aware of what could be happening for the better, and having too strong a feeling of "mission accomplished" takes the edge off of those vital thought processes that creates opportunities to improve. This is not to say successes shouldn't be celebrated. In fact, it's important to take time to recognize employees for their efforts and look for fun and creative ways to show recognition. It's just that it's equally important to keep our eyes on the ball so it doesn't bounce out of bounds while we are looking the other way.

So how can we keep our eyes on the ball? Fortunately, it's fairly easy to do. Look continuously for how to make even small adjustments to situations and procedures. This can be accomplished by having random conversations with managers— and mangers with their employees, as well as lead people within their work group about quality issues. A leader might ask what work situations do you "growl" about while driving to or from work? The leader may ask a simple question during a staff meeting like who has an idea for making an improvement that would make your job easier. I have found more often than not making small talk about "the little things" can lead to an improvement with something much bigger. Doing this also helps to support a mindset and culture of continuous improvement and a feeling of pride among all that comes from being a part of a high functioning operation.

Know Thyself

So, what else should Dave do in his assessment of the division. I said that Dave should learn about and understand his manager's strengths, areas for improvement, etc., but it's equally important for Dave to have a realistic view of his own strengths, traits, tendencies, and vulnerabilities. Dave should know things like under what circumstances he tends to respond favorably or not so favorably, or circumstances when he tends to procrastinate— or React too quickly. What situations is he comfortable handling, as well as those circumstances when he feels less equipped. Having such a realistic view is important for the same reason leaders should be aware of their managers' traits and tendencies. It's easy to take ourselves for granted and think we have it all pretty much together but not having a realistic and honest view of our own management style, traits, and capabilities creates limitations in us and a tendency to repeat our own mistakes.

Making a self-assessment may seem unnecessary and/or uncomfortable, but there are various relatively painless ways to do it with reasonable accuracy. The idea is to simply take a few minutes to stop and reflect honestly on one's successes as well as situations when we were less so. There are simple and free assessment techniques and tools online that can provoke thought about one's management style. Management team leaders may reach out to colleagues for objective feedback. If there is a particular trait or tendency that we have questions about, have a conversation about it with a trusted friend. Or, depending on the relationship, one may think about asking the boss. The irony in worrying about "exposing" one's self in this way is that many times what we may be worried about most has already been discovered by others. So, talking about it only works to one's advantage because it shows a certain honesty and willingness to make positive changes.

Leadership Profile

I use the term leadership profile to describe the recognition a leader enjoys regarding his/her personal credibility, style of management, and overall leadership capabilities. For example, a leader who is forward thinking, quality oriented, and has a history of resolving problems effectively and in a timely manner will be recognized by colleagues, upper management, and employees as having a strong management profile. One of the benefits of being recognized in this way is the boss and senior management are more likely to provide support when it is needed. Someone with a strong leadership profile is also more likely to get cooperation and support from colleagues who are willing to help with solving inter-department operations problems. Having a realistic view of one's own leadership profile is a part of knowing one's self and a step toward making adjustments that can benefit us in ways that may not be immediately apparent.

A Few Indicators of A Strong Leadership Profile

- Sets high performance and operations standards and expectations for self and his/her management team.
- Sets performance standards that are aligned with the organization's mission, objectives, and culture.
- Provides support through sound coaching and mentoring practices.
- Is an effective communicator and able to elicit support from others in order to meet reasonable objectives?
- Works effectively with HR representatives.
- Works effectively with managers and removes obstacles to help them achieve their specific objectives.
- Is recognized for being credible and trustworthy
- Is recognized as a resourceful problem solver

Separating the Diamonds from the Rough

Eventually, group leaders may need to recognize managers who do not meet performance standards and must face the unpleasant task of separation. It's important to begin this unpleasant process but avoiding it reduces the net competency and strength of the management team. It also reflects directly on the leader, and it reduces the management team's performance profile as a whole. In many cases not doing so also diminishes employee morale. But it needs to be accomplished with sensitivity and based on undeniable cause that demonstrates important deficiencies. In all of these cases, group leaders need to work with [their] boss and with the appropriate HR personnel to be sure of the process, the documentation, and reason [s] for taking this action are valid.

Keeping the Vision Alive

It is essential for group leaders to keep that central vision of management philosophy, process, and purpose alive and well. Leaders of any size work group need to create an environment where employees know the "ground rules", the expectations of performance, and have managers who are continuously looking to see where improvements can be made. Successful leaders are good at finding ways to tweak and modify processes so they can keep the idea of making progress alive. It also creates and reinforces a mindset within employees that helps to build pride in the workplace. The central objective here is to create a workplace environment that has all those holding lead positions looking, with their employees, for ways to improve. There needs to be a bottom up as well as top-down culture of ideas.

Organizations use posters and post clever phrases throughout work areas, but employees can also be encouraged to offer initiatives. I have seen employees create simple, interesting, and fun improvement initiatives that were later expanded and used throughout their division and facility.

I have found one way to foster such an environment is to set a few minutes aside during each staff meeting when managers– supervisors talk with their employees about quality and operations improvements. Perhaps the conversation can begin by asking employes during each meeting about what they have observed anywhere in the facility since the last meeting that supports– or is contrary to providing quality services or products. Doing so encourages conversation about real situations and opens opportunities for making improvements. I remember an employee talking about how chairs in their waiting room should be rearranged to provide their patients with a little greater sense of privacy. The employee saw how patients are seated in a small waiting room facing each other. After the meeting chairs were rearranged. This seemingly simple adjustment was a minor– almost not worthy thing to mention, but it was worthwhile for their patients and helped to reinforce a culture that spoke for the workplace as a whole.

Guard Against the Status Quo

I have observed an interesting and consistent characteristic with high-performing leaders. They always became uneasy when nothing new was happening. Where everyone seemed to feel good about things and when the "atmosphere" seemed to be a little too relaxed. A time when nothing new is happening seemed to trigger in them an urge to take another look around and make something happen. New art work on the walls. Fresh paint in a drab looking waiting area. Equipment that needs to be maintained a little more diligently. Something– anything too keep interest up! Highly successful leaders know that asking continuously what can we do to strengthen our organization or operation leads to a better place for all to work– and it strengthens the organization when its departments function in that way.

I have been fortunate to have opportunities to work with these high performing leaders who were able to, along with their many other more direct responsibilities, function as canaries in the mine. They always seem to see things others can't or don't wish to bother with. I find it interesting that although a few of these individuals were clearly Type A personalities others were much more moderated in style but their common internal drive and ability to "keep the ball rolling" was undeniable.

Reward and Recognition

Everyone looks forward to getting recognition and everyone in a leadership position should look for ways to satisfy this expectation of our human nature. Formal recognition usually comes at specific times after a project has been completed successfully. Sometimes recognition comes with something tangible, a certificate, a plaque, or a gift. But a simple informal and well-timed "well done" or "thank you" can also show genuine appreciation for a smart or particularly thoughtful action. Genuine informal expressions of appreciation like these from leaders are powerful and they build morale throughout the workplace.

Humor

Humor and allowing for levity are essential ingredients to providing leadership, it's not a luxury. Using humor or some manner of levity works to strengthen collegiality within a management group and among employees. Leaders can use humor in many ways. It can be used intelligently and appropriately to address various circumstances that would have been difficult to approach otherwise. It can be used to relieve tension from various situations, and it can redirect energy by creating a momentary break that works to clear the air, or tension. It can be used wisely to put aside in a "forgiving or understanding way" a well-intended but not so successful effort by a manager or employee.

Leaders who have difficulty with mustering a "funny bone" may be fortunate enough to have someone in their work group who's sense of timing can be relied upon occasionally to find a little levity in a situation. But humor should not be used as a vehicle for sarcasm or ridicule, especially toward someone, no matter how strongly one may feel. I have seen leaders use this kind of humor and the results were always negative. The uneasy chuckles such humor is expected to evoke was short lived while its more negative nature had a longer shelf life. Leaders who use sarcasm or dark humor routinely risk revealing more about themselves than the person or situation they targeted.

Disarming the Sacred Cow

There are few things more discouraging to a cohesive and high-functioning management team or group of employees than sustaining the efforts of the "sacred cow" member whose word seems to carry a self-imagined and disproportionate weight. This is especially true when those individuals seem to assume it to be their role. Management teams almost always have members with unique training and specific skill sets such as finance, personnel, facilities, compliance, etc., Their points of view, council, and opinions need to take the lead when those topics are on the table, but when someone consistently moves to dominate with their opinion on virtually any topic, the leader needs to disarm their imagined import.

Group leaders can balance this by making a point to ask or challenge others on the team for their thoughts about what is being discussed or propose alternate ideas for all to comment. The group leader's responsibility in these circumstances is to make sure everyone feels they have equal stake in the discussion. But at other times, leaders may need to take more direct action by having a private discussion with the person.

Chapter Summary

Characteristics of a high functioning team leader include:

➢ Having a clear and realistic view of operations, personnel, and objectives

➢ Works toward creating a safe collegial environment that encourages open to two-way communication

➢ Establishes a commitment among management team members to maintain a uniformly high standard of performance

➢ Supports an environment where managers are able to function as an employee sounding board to the group leader

➢ Establish a well-grounded vision of process, purpose, philosophies and techniques

➢ An ability to recognize managers' individual strengths and limitations and can employ appropriate coaching and guidance when needed

➢ Be willing to support managers with the idea that an *errant initiative or failed outcome may be less important than a manager's unwillingness to experience the effort or be unable to learn from it"*

➢ Uses humor appropriately

➢ Be cautious about the "mission accomplished" mindset

➢ Keep on the look-out for something new

THREE ESSENTIAL LEADERSHIP TRAITS, MANAGING EMPLOYEE EXPECTATIONS, INTERVIEWING MANAGEMENT CANDIDATES MANAGING TIME

The Mule and the Purchaser

A man wished to purchase a mule, and agreed with its owner that he should try out the animal before he bought him. He took the mule home and put him in the straw-yard with his

other mules, upon which the new animal left all the others and at once joined the one that was most idle and the greatest eater of them all. Seeing this, the man put a halter on him and led him back to his owner. On being asked how, in so short a time, he could have made a trial of him, he answered, "I do not need a trial; I know that he will be just the same as the one he chose for his companion."

A Man Is Known by the Company He Keeps

Practical Application

Successful leaders attract, identify, and hire candidates who demonstrate critical leadership traits and employees who can bring quality and character to their organization.

Case Study

After six months on her new job, Ellen could claim virtually no improvement with the performance of her employees or with the department's inefficiencies. She was genuinely puzzled about this because her previous ten years of management experience had been successful. She also began to sense her new boss maybe questioning her effectiveness. It was clearly time for Ellen to reassess her approach, evaluate her performance and management tactics, and do a thorough department assessment with her supervisors.

Discussion

The "wellness" of an operation is almost always a reflection of its manager's ability to manage and his/her management priorities. All workplace operations experience difficulties from time to time but when the frequency of issues moves from being an exception to predictable or not surprising its leader needs to be at the forefront of evaluating cause and making changes for the better. Blaming employees as we saw in Chapter one is at most only a partial answer. Circumstances where employees function poorly don't evolve on their own. Someone hired those "bad apples" and someone allowed them to evolve to a point where they are influencing operations. Sometimes things occur that are truly beyond a managers control, but many times they are within the manager's control and were allowed to continue. Emily may have been delt a tough hand to play with her new job but she knew from past experience that positive changes can be made even with the most difficult scenarios. She had to stop and figure out what is different with her current assignment.

Emily has to take charge of the situation, not point blame, and overcome the feeling of being overwhelmed. She can begin by asking relevant questions that will lead to her seeing why she is having so little progress. She knew the [fix] lays with her and that the big question is where to start. Fortunately, Emily's boss, Patrick understood the difficulties so Emily was able to have helpful conversations with him and get the guidance she needed. After having a few frank discussions she was able to better understand the department's history and see how the current situation evolved, which provided clues to some of the solutions. Now, she must make accurate and well targeted assessments of the current circumstances and in as short a time as possible, implement new action plans.

I inherited a similar situation early in my management career. One day as I was talking to my boss about all the difficulties and challenges that I inherited as he reached to his desk drawer and placed a stuffed monkey on the desk. I continued. He then reached down a second time to get a small palm size stone and put it next to the monkey. He put his hand up to stop me and said simply; "I'm not going to take this monkey off your back. It's yours to deal with, but I am going to do everything I can to move the rocks out of your way." That simple gesture and comment was all I needed to understand. I had no doubt from that point forward where I stood with him and my job description. He kept his word and eventually I found my way to making substantial operations improvements. I found his coaching philosophy to be one that I would adopt and apply with my leadership roles thereafter. Blaming the circumstances is simply not part of a leader's job description.

Fortunately, Emily's boss understood her first task was to make an accurate assessment of the cause-and-effect and avoid reacting to the symptoms she recognized early on. Solutions to virtually all management situations come from collecting and validating information, evaluating it with an open mind, and carefully filtering that information through a root cause assessment process. This may seem at first to be time-consuming, a too regimented and "over the top" process especially with situations that seem relatively simple, but it doesn't have to be excessive and the benefits are always greater than if the effort is side stepped and it can be accomplished within a much shorter time than one might imagine. But it requires exercising keen observation skills and knowing who to talk with and how to ask questions while making no assumptions. Asking different people the same question [why] until the circumstance can be validated is important.

In this situation the problems were long-standing and involved more than 80 employees. Emily and Patrick felt outside help was indicated. Fortunately, the organization's HR department had trained counsellors who were available to help, and Harriet was asked to assist. The assessment began with Harriet meeting with employees to get their views on the various problems. As expected with the first employee meeting, the conversation began with employees pointing to Emily as being the problem. Several charges were leveled at their previous manager as well and they began to see Emily in the same light. The employes said work is not being distributed fairly and Emily is too harsh and even arbitrary when counselling or disciplining employees. There were several other complaints about her allowing the work area to be cluttered and disorganized, which caused waisted time. They said procedures were not consistently followed and employees had varying skill levels which they contributed to work assignments not being distributed fairly. But predictably, other employees supported Emily as a hard working well intended manager who was overloaded with her own duties.

As Harriet and Emily reviewed their notes from the employee meeting, Emily described her frustration with her workload. She also said a few of her 80 FTE workgroup had formed [clicks] and seemed to be more interested in challenging her than helping to make changes for the better. Along with the employee clicks, Emily described a few other employees who were particularly troublesome because of their marginal skills. A follow up meeting with the employees was scheduled and Harriet and Emily took time to recognize and address specific employee complaints. They also made a point to say Emily agreed with many of their concerns and would refocus her effort to address those issues. Emily told everyone that she will begin working with her supervisors to improve 5 of the most discussed issues.

Later, Emily talked with her shift supervisors about how their management problems could be more clearly defined, prioritized and addressed. Emily could see the five issues they want to address were functional issues not people specific problems and talked about finding a new approach to what they were doing. A short time later Emily met with Harriet and described a draft of the new action plan she developed with her supervisors which was implemented successfully.

We sometimes hear that it is the little things that mean a lot. In fact, it can be the one little thing that triggers the final employee reaction that brings unrest to a head, and this case study is a good example. Their problems evolved slowly over time so it was difficult to see the unrecognized issues accumulate slowly until a single small incident about reassigning an employee triggered the feeling among employees that [everything] is wrong. Operations and personnel problems often evolve slowly and even innocently so it is difficult for managers to recognize their affect.

One reason for this slow burn is because employees and her managers made adjustments willingly to overcome [what should have been noted and corrected] and without realizing their omission to correct, created opportunities for secondary problems to evolve. For example, depending on a few willing employees to perform certain tasks rather than distributing the workload evenly can build resentment over time. It may have been better to fix a possible competency problem or address unwilling employees rather than compensate by expecting other more willing employees to perform a task.

Two Key Dimensions of Management

Range of Accountability
and
Threshold for Taking Action

Being Pressed by Time

Managers have a wide range of responsibilities which makes it difficult to keep all those balls from bouncing out of bounds. Because of the many routine desk tasks along with a continuous stream of interruptions and challenges, managers tend to prioritize [on the fly] and balance what needs to be done now, tomorrow, or perhaps sometime later. It's an important survival technique that helps us get through the day. The problem, of course, is this kind of prioritizing impacts the operation in ways we can't see. It's easy to simply loss track of the commitment to address something tomorrow and then is forgotten altogether as other new issues evolve. This, of course, is what often allows for the accumulation of the "little things"— and the employees thinking their manager is not in touch with what's happening or simply doesn't care. These issues may not be a manager's immediate problem, but they [are] immediate day to day issues for their employees. The instigator of this, of course, is time. Taking enough time to fix [everything] [perfectly] [all the time] is an incredibly daunting notion and virtually impossible task to achieve.

However, there are solutions to this dilemma that will be addressed in more detail throughout this writing. But for the sake of this discussion, I want to look at something that can help at any level of leadership. It's a process of sorting through and giving order to an array of those [little] accumulating issues. It's what I refer to as the Scope of Responsibility and Threshold for Taking Action.

Scope of Responsibility

Scope of responsibility helps us focus on the wide range of operating issues that are within a manager's responsibility. Scope of responsibility helps to make us more aware of all the pieces of one's operation that directly impact efficiencies and quality of service/product— but are the little things and often out of a manager's sight. Here are just a few examples.

- Availability of supplies, equipment, and other items that employees depend on minute by minute to do their jobs.
- Having a staffing plan that provides fair coverage on all the shifts

- Cleanliness and orderliness of the workplace
- Attention given to employee training, along with clearly defined competency standards or performance expectations.
- Attention given to employee recognition and morale issues
- Availability and clarity of instruction manuals

It is surprising how many of these items are given less priority as managers attend to their immediate duties against available time. But in this case study we see that Emily's employees thought of them as high priority items. As minor or incidental as any one of these may have appeared to Emily, they had a real effect on Emily's employees. I can't tell you how many staff meetings I attended as a casual observer over the years hearing employees complain about how such small things were being overlooked by their manager while their managers seemed completely puzzled about their employee's "random" complaints. Sometimes describing them as "just whining".

Scope of Accountability includes the day-to-day things that a manager or supervisor can reasonably control, such as those listed above. Making such a list may seem unnecessary and too time consuming. But it can be useful for one important reason. It brings those items that may have been inadvertently given a low priority or forgotten into clear focus with proper priority. Maybe such a list can come by asking a single or small group of employees to list all the things they depend on to do their jobs.

Or, one could walk through the workplace for the specific purpose of making mental notes about the effort employees put into simple tasks, take notice of how the equipment they use is performing, or see in detail how they are performing their tasks. Another way is to take the initiative and ask employees during a meeting about things they would like to see improved or change to make their jobs easier to perform. Doing this goes a long way to putting the small things back on the radar screen and lets the employees know that their leader is interested in helping them do the best job they can. It takes little effort and time. Doing this once or perhaps twice a year can benefit managers as well as the employees. And, in a long run it works to reduce a manager's stress because it helps to prevent small problems accumulate.

Threshold for Taking Action

The second dimension I refer to is the threshold for taking corrective action. In other words, at what point does personnel conduct or system dysfunction trigger a manager to take corrective action. As we observe the workplace, we sometimes see variations from what we know should be happening. The question that comes to mind is, does this need to be addressed now and if not, how much latitude should it be given before something is done about it. Sometimes, something may occur that is clearly outside of the established standard and action needs to be taken promptly or within a short term. It's important for a manager to have a realistic view of his/her own threshold for taking action. I have been involved with workplaces where the manager had become accustomed to giving wide latitude while viewing performance issues, then being surprised later when a combination of these issues caused a new situation.

When corrective action is taken, it's important to be consistent with where those thresholds are set for a given circumstance. I have seen managers take action inconsistently for the same performance variance which causes confusion and sometimes resentment as employees see the same action handled differently among employees.

People can't be expected to function perfectly all the time and managers can't take action every time a variance occurs, but some managers are recognized as being relaxed and tolerant while others are less so. The point is we would be wise to stop occasionally and make an assessment of what's happening in the workplace with respect to reinforcing performance standards and become aware of our tolerances.

When reasonable thresholds are set and acted upon in a <u>timely</u> and <u>consistent</u> way personnel performance, quality of service, and efficiency improves. Employees like having clear and consistent criteria for measuring performance because it provides boundaries for them that works to reduce on-the-job stress. It works to provide a safe "playground" where employees can function without question.

Delegating the [Little Things]

Let's think about the time that is needed for doing [everything perfectly– all the time]. Time is a leading cause of stress among managers. So, managers must take advantage of opportunities to delegate. Instead of taking on the burden of keeping everything functioning perfectly ourselves, let's think about another approach. I say this because in many instances employees are not only willing, but happy to help solve problems that can make their work easier. Why not have them help?

For example, with Emily's 80 employees, she was able to have 6 volunteers work on specific tasks. Two worked on updating and organizing two procedure books with guidance from their supervisor. Two others were assigned to create a procedure for having instruments and various supply items always available in the work areas. In this case, they worked directly with Emily to establish new rules that would help keep the area organized and supplies immediately available. Her employees complained about those issues and were happy to get involved with doing something that would make their work easier.

Two other employees agreed to manage the inventory and they recommended and implemented a new procedure for ordering supplies which kept the inventory updated. The volunteers were given time during staff meetings to update everyone on their tasks which gave them recognition and made them feel good about what they were doing to benefit everyone. Everyone was able to see progress and the complaints about Emily not paying attention to their immediate needs subsided. Not all of the workplace issues were completely resolved, but it created a better environment that allowed Emily more time to move ahead and focus on her immediate tasks and do so with less stress.

The remaining problem about the skill level needed to be addressed so Emily and her supervisors took time to implement a retraining program which helped to solve the task distribution concerns.

Three Critical Leadership Traits

We saw in Chapter One the need for building a strong management team. This chapter focuses on individual manager performance and three leadership traits that I believe are among the most critical. The three traits I'm referring to are: intellect, wisdom, and commonsense. First, intellect. We tend to equate intellect with simply being "smart" academically. But Webster describes intelligence as "the ability to learn or understand or deal with new or trying situations." Webster further defines it as "The ability to apply knowledge to manipulate one's environment or to think abstractly ." These two explanations also fit perfectly to describe a manager's capabilities which I refer to as *management acumen*. Those definitions fit nicely into the topic of leadership because assessing, dealing with circumstances, and manipulating [managing] workplace situations are the primary responsibilities of leadership at any level. Management acumen includes two other traits of effective leadership, and they are wisdom and commonsense. I believe these three traits are essential and work together to drive virtually all of the critical thinking processes leaders must employ.

I see intellect, within the context of this discussion, as the ability to think clearly through and consider a maze of distractions, issues, and symptoms in order to recognize the essential finding, [root cause]. Staying at the surface of a problem and focusing on its symptoms is convenient and tantalizing, but it is counter-productive and in the long run, a waste of time. Under the best scenario, it may show some immediate gains but, in most cases, no long-term solutions. The capacity of a manager to make sound decisions in a timely manner and make insightful assessments are clear indicators of leadership acumen.

Wisdom is the second of these critical traits. I view wisdom to be the ability to visualize or anticipate accurately the outcome of one's action over other possible actions. In a practical sense, I believe wisdom is gained by having the ability to learn from past experiences and from making insightful [intelligent] observations. Exercising wisdom is important because it helps one see outcomes from an array possible actions or decisions. Wisdom is also gained from having the opportunity to work with successful leaders.

The third element is commonsense, which is simply doing what complies with the expectations that are embedded in our human nature. I find it interesting that given the variations in personalities, intellect, and capabilities that are distributed among us all, there always seems to be a constant consensus on things that simply "make sense". There are no defined rules about what makes sense, but when something just seems right to us we recognize it uniformly as being "sensible", or on the other hand, "ridiculous". Exercising our ability to function in a "commonsense fashion" is essential to providing strong and effective leadership, and I believe the good news here is that often times exercising our commonsense leads us to make the simplest and most effective decisions. Another benefit of being recognized as a smart, wise, and commonsense person is that we are considered to be "safe" to work with. It helps to build alliances and garners support among colleagues.

As I mentioned above, there are other useful traits and skills for exercising effective leadership that can be described, but clearly there no substitutes for this trifecta of leadership traits. The curious thing about "common" sense also is that we often think that it isn't that common after all. So why is it that people in leadership situations who seem to be wise and smart enough don't show these three traits at times? My view is that it's often because of the other pressures that might be driving circumstances. When caught in situations we may view as threatening or pressured, it can lead one to do something out of character, so there seems to be a certain fragility with these three traits and it seems to depend on one's own constitution for listening to [that little voice inside] that is telling us the "right" thing to do, while being aware that we can be swad by circumstances.

We sometimes hear an essential trait of strong and effective leaders is the willingness to take risks, which I don't dispute in any way. But, being willing to take risks does not contradict or is the abandonment of using our intellect, wisdom, and commonsense. In fact, I believe it is using those three traits which allows us to assess risks and take of advantages of opportunities successfully.

Interviewing and Selecting Managers

This chapter is also about selecting candidates for various management positions at virtually all levels. The fable in this chapter raises a question about the filtering process we use to select a candidate for a management or another level of leadership position. First, we need to be aware that in most instances interviewers usually, and unwittingly, use their own traits to filter and gauge a candidate's strength, limitations, and leadership acumen. A simple example of this is a [smart] interviewer will most often select a candidate who he/she views as being smart. An interviewer who demonstrates commonsense will look for and select a candidate who can demonstrate that same trait. It's why leaders, who have this trifecta of traits, are more likely to hire their direct reports who have these traits, and have highly successful operations.

If what we see in a candidate coincides with who [we are], that candidate is more likely to be viewed as a top contender. Likewise, supervisors will employ the same filtering process when they interview candidates for first line employee positions. I have heard an interviewer say, "It was *that one* thing the candidate said that made the decision for me". I believe that candidate was hired almost certainly because *that one* comment by the interviewee happed to coincide strongly with one of the interviewer's own strong traits. I believe this is more than a coincidental happening, it helps to explain why managers with certain traits eventually create a division of managers who have those same characteristics.

The fable above shows this in a humorous way, but it also makes a valid point when interviewing. Here are a few of my own. The first is to understand the candidate's thinking processes. How does he/ she tend to react to various circumstances? Are they pragmatic? What is their baseline strategy for dealing with personnel or operations issues? Thinking back to Chapter 1, how does the candidate view their employees? Is the candidate detail oriented? To what degree are they compulsive and can be depended upon to do the "right" thing consistently? Do they mainly think analytically or by intuition?

I certainly want to know if the candidate can demonstrate the three essential management traits in some way. I'll ask about how the candidate would address and resolve certain situations. Maybe use actual situations that are taken from the organization's own past or current operation. If the candidate begins by focusing on symptoms and goes on to describe action steps, I'll be concerned. I'm not looking for solutions to symptoms, I want to know about cause. I would be more interested in a candidate who talks about the symptoms as I described them but then goes on to suggest a possible underlying issues. If a candidate's conversation seems to meander without a semblance of direction for fact finding I'm turned off.

I may ask the candidate about expense budgets. I'll ask how he/ she prepares for the coming year's budget. If the candidate immediately talks about expenses– a yellow flag goes up. That may be part of the answer in some circumstances but I want to know if any notes were taken during the current year while at meetings with discussions that could impact the new year's operating budget. Meetings occur throughout the year with other department heads and senior management when changes in policy, process, new programs, or regulatory requirements are discussed. Some of those conversations are bound to influence a given department's coming year's operating budget and those situations need to be accounted for when preparing for next year's budget. The same with random conversations in the corridors about changes colleagues are making in their departments. A candidate who shows forethought like that gets my immediate attention. Candidates for management positions who can demonstrate strong communication skills are attention getters. Candidates who can in some way show they have an interest in what's happening on the floor and understand the relationship between happy employees and good operations outcomes are also attention getters. Overriding all of these characteristics and traits is the need to recognize a candidate's personal credibility and integrity.

I might ask a candidate a question like, does he/she feel understanding human nature helps when working with employ situations? I believe it's an important question because our human nature's expectations set virtually all the ground rules for how people act, react, and expect to be treated by their manager. The candidate may not be thinking in terms of "human nature" specifically but I want to know what [things] he or she feels are important when working with employees and colleagues. Using a wide range of questions like these helps to gauge a candidate's thinking processes and gives important clues to how they will most likely react to various situations. In addition to getting answers to these questions, it's useful to see how a candidate manages his/her answers. Are they sufficiently confident or over confident– or less so?

Depending on a position's specific responsibilities, gauging a candidate's technical skills is equally important so the interviewer needs to balance the technical requirements of the job with the broad scope of interview questions that are given above.

Human Nature, Using the Power of Leadership

At seminars we commonly hear different versions of the idea "people first". But what does that mean? Employees are our most important and often most expensive resources and we know high morale among employees leads to a smoother-running more cost-efficient workplace. The question is how can we achieve that level of performance and keep employees happy. Or, how can we make employees happy and content without losing control.

Recognizing human nature and how it's expectations can be reasonably satisfied is important because how those expectations are managed drives virtually all employee behavior. Managers at all levels who can recognize this and apply this reality to their decision making are less confused with their employee's reactions and are able to anticipate and manage those reactions more effectively. Here are a few characteristics of those expectations that can help managers manage.

1. Human nature's expectations are embedded uniformly in our employees [and] within all of us
2. When those expectations are satisfied or aggravated, the reaction is predictable
3. Human nature's expectations haven't changed over the past thousands of years and are not likely to change in the foreseeable future

These three characteristics help managers because it establishes predictable ground rules for leaders at all levels for managing situationsand helps us anticipate the outcome of actions and decisions.

Organizations/Managers are from Mars—Employees are from Venus

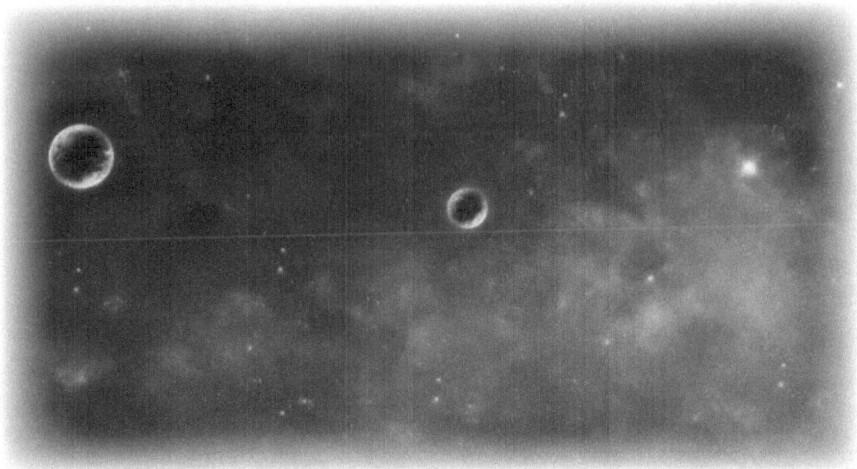

Let's take this discussion about human nature one more step and consider the idea that like people, organizations have a nature of their own, and predictably an accompanying set of expectations. An organizations' expectations materialize in the form of mission statements, vision, goals, objectives, policies, and procedures, and these elements of an organization's nature trickle down to establish a set of rules that employees– and their managers are expected to honor in the workplace.

So, on one hand, we have a set of expectations that are driven by our human nature and on the other is a set of expectations that are driven by the organization's nature. The problem, of course, with this scenario is that these two sets of expectations are not always aligned and the effect of this leads to conflicts and misunderstandings. Let's look at a few examples. Our human nature drives us to be creative and exercise our individuality, and we have strong need to exercise free will. We also feel a need to have control of our environment which helps us feel safe and secure. But, the nature of an organization, through its policies seeks to control us, which can create a kind of pressure of will between employees and their organization. Fortunately, in most cases this miss alignment can be managed often with insightful leadership.

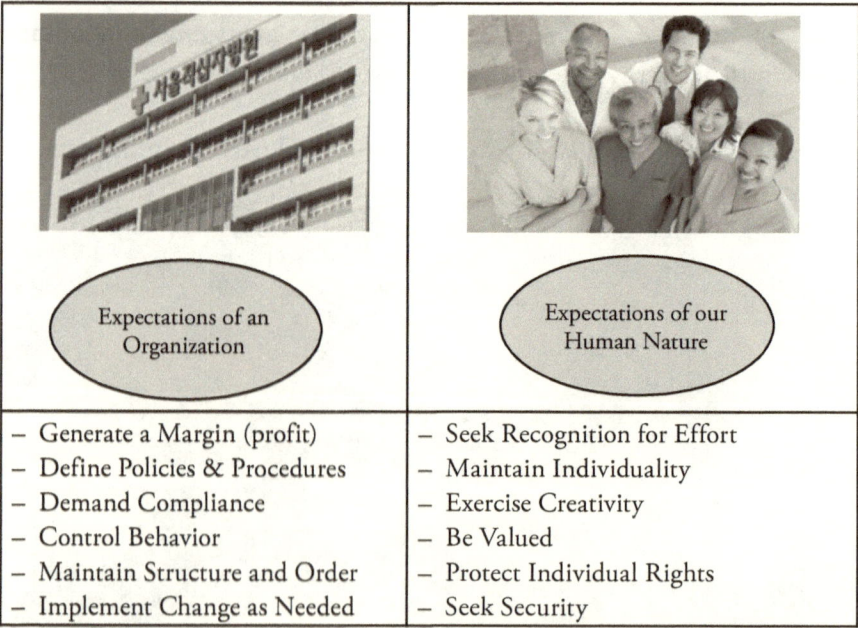

Expectations of an Organization	Expectations of our Human Nature
– Generate a Margin (profit)	– Seek Recognition for Effort
– Define Policies & Procedures	– Maintain Individuality
– Demand Compliance	– Exercise Creativity
– Control Behavior	– Be Valued
– Maintain Structure and Order	– Protect Individual Rights
– Implement Change as Needed	– Seek Security

But, even in the best of circumstances managing these differences can be challenging. The first step managers need to take is to understand these two opposing sets of expectations are legitimate [on their own] and each needs to be navigated with intellect, wisdom, and commonsense. I want to be clear that doing so does not mean pandering employees or being soft or minimize an organization's authority or its expectations. But it does mean that it is worth the Effort to account for employee's basic expectations. And doing this does not contradict setting high performance standards. In fact, they are very compatible. The point here is to recognize the idea of *people first* simply means being willing to account for employees' basic expectations. Practicing the notion of people first in leadership can have a very positive impact on the success of an organization.

Finding the Diamond in the Rough

When considering applications for management positions I don't want to overlook those "diamonds in the rough" who populate virtually every organization. Once found, they can become valuable additions to an organization's management team. I had a few opportunities to find these individuals, but one in particular comes to mind. Without going into all of the details, this employee was a part timer who worked the late weekend shift in the ER for only six months. Her name came as a casual comment from a coworker during one of my rounds. I took the bait and later asked for the employee to stop by and talk for a few minutes about how things are going on her shift. We talked briefly and I asked her to tell me how she would describe her workplace environment. The conversation broadened and I began to recognize some of the management traits I know to be crucial. We began to talk in a little more detail about one or two of the situation's she described and as the conversation continued, I began to realized she was also a very insightful person.

After a few days of interviewing other outside very capable candidates for a management spot that had opened a month earlier, I thought more seriously about the conversation I had with the part time ER employee. The only additional feedback I got was that she was well liked and demonstrated a good work ethic. I was feeling uneasy about considering her for managing a department with more than 100 people, especially since she had no prior management experience. It was a busy department, but I also felt I had to trust my instincts. After thinking about this more, I asked her to talk with me in more detail about the idea of managing a large group of employees. I also talked with my boss about the risks of hiring this neophyte. He agreed I should follow my instincts and make an offer, and the decision turned out to be one of best personnel decisions I've ever made.

She proved to have the traits and leadership characteristics the situation needed. She was also very coachable and within six months on the job I could see that operations in her department were beginning to move in the right direction. Although the feedback from a few of her employees was mixed at times, the overall feeling was weighed heavily in her favor. This is an extreme example, but it makes the point that candidates like this populate virtually all organizations and deserve opportunities for advancement. Organizations that have programs to recognize these employees and provide appropriate training for them can realize huge benefits. Her confidence grew along with her gradual successes and that sense of confidence allowed her to use appropriate flexibility when the situation was right which her employees appreciated.

Evaluating Candidates for Supervisory and Management Positions

1. Basic information.
    a. Type of facility, organization, or circumstance where the candidate is currently employed. [determines fit]
    b. How long has the candidate held management positions
    c. How many people does a manager oversee.
    d. What type of services did the candidate's workgroup provide. [determines how those experiences translate to the open position]
    e. Current operating budget responsibilities, successes and failures in holding to the budget. [what process does the candidate use to prepare budgets]
2. What are two important things the candidate learned about providing sound leadership? [consider the things candidates believe are important to employees.]
3. Ask about how the candidate manages stress, and about specific circumstances that can trigger stress.

4. Ask the candidate to talk about two things that led to employee and manager disconnects? [helps to assess the candidates' understanding of employee expectations]

5. Would the candidate discuss one or two examples of what managers can do to build a workplace environment where employee morale and quality of performance is high? Is it possible to have one without the other? Get examples.

6. What are the candidate's expectations of his/her boss.

   a. What kinds of things can the candidate do to help build a positive working relationship with the boss, and vice versa? [consider the candidate's fit with your performance expectations, work style, and management philosophy]

7. Ask the candidate to talk about an operations or personnel problem he/she had to resolve?

   a. How did the candidate research the situation?

   b. What needed to be corrected and what action led to the solution? [Helps to assess if the candidate's approach fits with the organization's culture].

8. Ask the candidate to talk about key accomplishments and why they were important.

9. Ask the candidate to describe three important employee expectations.

10. What does the candidate feel are among the most important things to do when communicating with employees and colleagues. [helps to determine a willingness to be open and have two-way conversations with employees and colleagues]

11. Ask the candidate about what he/she can do to help align employees' effort with the organization's vision and objectives.

Determine how much mentoring or training the candidate may need. Consider personality fit, awareness of self, level of self-confidence, credibility the candidate generates.

■ Chapter Summary

- ➤ Department managers and supervisors need to have a realistic vision of their;
  - o Management style
  - o Philosophy regarding employees
- ➤ Be aware of the Two Dimensions of Management
  - o Scope of Accountability
  - o Threshold for Taking Action
- ➤ Consider the benefit of delegating tasks to employees who volunteer
- ➤ Recognize the need to manage the organization's expectations with those of the employees
- ➤ Assess the technical skills to the degree that is appropriate for the job.
- ➤ Look for the three key leadership traits when interviewing candidates for management, supervisory– and first line positions.
- ➤ Watch for and evaluate [in house] talent for leadership positions.
- ➤ Don't hesitate to take notes when interviewing.

CHAPTER THREE

CONFLICT MANAGEMENT

The Man, the Boy, and the Donkey

A Man and his son were once going with their Donkey to market. As they were walking along by its side a countryman passed them and said: "You fools, what is a Donkey for but to ride upon?"

So the Man put the Boy on the Donkey and they went on their way. But soon they passed a group of men, one of whom said: "See that lazy youngster, he lets his father walk while he rides."

So the Man ordered his Boy to get off, and got on himself. But they hadn't gone far when they passed two women, one of whom said to the other: "Shame on that lazy lout to let his poor little son trudge along."

Well, the Man didn't know what to do, but at last he took his Boy up before him on the Donkey. By this time they had come to the town, and the passers-by began to jeer and point at them. The Man stopped and asked what they were scoffing at. The men said: "Aren't you ashamed of yourself for overloading that poor donkey of you and your hulking son?"

The Man and Boy got off and tried to think what to do. They thought and they thought, till at last they cut down a pole, tied the donkey's feet to it, and raised the pole and the donkey to their shoulders. They went along amid the laughter of all who met them till they came to Market Bridge, when the Donkey, getting one of his feet loose, kicked out and caused the Boy to drop his end of the pole. In the struggle the Donkey fell over the bridge, and his fore-feet being tied together he was drowned.

Please all, and you will please none.

Practical Application

Trying to please one, a group, or all impedes using leadership and most often leads to additional complications.

Case Study

Joan has been managing her work group for several years. She is a friendly person and a solid manager and her department provides high-quality customer service. She is conscientious about training her staff and uses sound judgment to direct operations. However, new demands for services required her to formulate a new work schedule. To this point, the workgroup had been able to close their department for lunch break and enjoy having lunch together, but their new volume made this practice difficult to continue and additional coverage hours were needed because the workload on the evening and weekend shifts increased.

Joan was able to hire additional staff to work the new slots, and their long-standing and highly valued lunch schedule had to be abandoned and was replaced with rotating staff. These changes soon began to cause Controversy and Joan had to make hard decisions about how to reset the long-standing practices her employees had enjoyed.

Her senior employees felt strongly that they should have priority of shifts on the new schedule. After all, it was their effort, time, and competencies that helped bring the department to its current level of success. But the less senior people felt their individual roles and responsibilities would contribute equally to the new services and felt favoring senior people is unfair to them. Both senior and less senior employees had worked well together to this time; however, the new situation became contentious and Joan felt more and more pressure to find a resolution. Joan was at a loss to reconcile and make a decision for fear of angering and losing the support and loyalty of the senior group who she considered to be high-performing and who she depended on to perform the more complex procedures. But she also didn't want to lose the support of her less senior people.

Discussion

Trying to please an individual or group of employees while trying to meet new performance standards can lead to a variety of complications and added stress for the manager. Both groups of employees felt they had reasonable expectations regarding scheduling but those expectations were conflicting and it was up to Joan to sort it out while staying focused on her primary responsibility– holding to clearly defined operations objectives. Joan also needed to be careful to not show favoritism. These situations are laden with traps of all sorts but Joan's delayed decision-making increased speculation and put more pressure on herself. Unfortunately, there are no hard-and-fast rules for addressing these situations, but there are a few points that can help provide some direction.

First, before making a decision Joan needs to commit to maintaining open communication with [all] her employees and be willing to explore reasonable options for a resolution. In these situations, there is sometimes a tendency to talk only with those who are more "friendly" with the manager. The air can be tense during these times, but despite that, Joan needs to focus everyone's thinking on specific operational requirements and objectives and not on her employes' emotions. Second, she needs to recognize that asking employees for suggestions does not mean she is retreating from her decision-making responsibilities. She has the final say and all decisions will remain with Joan. She is in charge and that doesn't change when allowing employees to openly discuss their concerns and points of view. Doing so always helps everyone better understand the *core issues and requirements of the service* which they were employed to provide. It's up to Joan to make those points clear in the minds of her employees. The organization's primary objective is to provide high quality customer services or high-quality products, and that is what gives grounding to Joan's decision making.

Employees may not like the outcome but they will at least recognize their manager's willingness to listen to alternatives, suggestions, and allow for a measure of latitude if possible. If Joan holds to that line of thinking she can more easily shift her focus from the employee's individual issues to service objectives– without losing all of their support. Before Joan talks with her employees and asks for alternate solutions, she needs to be clear with herself and them on where the boundaries are when considering suggestions so the discussion can be managed from the very beginning.

Listening to employees who live the everyday details of their jobs can point out less obvious but important things about the workplace which could be helpful to Joan's decision making. With regards to taking employee's suggestions, I found that they are most often realistic– and sometimes even more conservative than what their manager may be considering. Employees know that allowing for too much latitude may give some of their coworkers an opportunity to "game" the system in their favor.

The point here is having open and frank communication that is focused on clear operations objectives is essential especially when trying to resolve contentious situations. It also keeps employees from editorializing the issues in their favor or miss understanding the core reason [s] for making decision[s]. One can feel lonely while thinking through and navigating these situations, but the process of decision making doesn't have to be a lonely one with good communication.

Being Alert to Problems

Having managed more than a few conflict scenarios I have come to understand it's the supervisor or manager's mindset that can determine how discussions with employees will play out. I have seen situations when a manager's mindset [attitude] and temperament worked to either incite or moderate employee reaction and willingness to understand and cooperate. Our attitudes can lead us to using a certain tone when speaking, body language, or choice of words that can send unintended signals. Employees are keen to pick up and use these signals to determine their own reactions. Managers always need to be aware of their mindset– especially when tensions are high so they can avoid these communication landmines. I have seen managers be completely unaware of how they are approaching a discussion. It is always helpful to stop and take a moment to do a self-check before having these discussions in order to create the best possible scenario for sending the right message and gaining cooperation.

Also, take the time before hand to understand and validate everyone's points of view. Discussing things that have been validated puts a leader in a much better position than arguing with employees about assumptions or impressions. A key objective is to get everyone or at least as many as possible thinking in the same way about the realities of a situation. A durable decision needs to satisfy five basic criteria; knowing the facts, having them clearly defined, interpreting them correctly, staying focused on the central issue, and maintaining good communication. Paying attention to the peripherals is distracting and has little value in finding solutions.

Chapter Summary

- ➢ Decision making can be lonely at times, but the process that leads to a decision doesn't have to be lonely.
- ➢ The first criteria for reaching a decision is to satisfy the *needs of the operation*. Once those needs are defined the second criteria is to appropriately address the basic expectations of the employees.
    - ○ Satisfy expectations for building as much equity into the decision as possible.
    - ○ Avoid the appearance of favoritism.
    - ○ Maintain open two-way communication. Employees expect to be informed and kept up to date on where things stand and what they can expect to happen next.
- ➢ Review and objectively evaluate all reasonable suggestions regardless of the source.
    - ○ Be aware of underlying motives of those suggesting alternatives and how their suggestions suggestions will impact the outcome.
- ➢ Preview the decision with supervisors and get feedback from those who are directly involved.
- ➢ Communicate and implement the decision. Tell why alternatives solutions are acceptable and not acceptable.
    - ○ Reinforce the need for compliance.
    - ○ Be clear about your commitment to enforce the decision.
- ➢ Keep the boss up dated.
- ➢ Provide training if indicated and other underpinning issues.

CHAPTER FOUR

DEVELOPING STRONG COMMUNICATION SKILLS

The Eagle and Arrow

An Eagle was soaring through the air when suddenly it heard the whizz of an Arrow, and felt itself wounded to death. Slowly it fluttered down to the earth, with its life-blood pouring out of it. Looking down upon the Arrow with which it had been pierced, it found that the shaft of the Arrow had been feathered with one of its own plumes.

"Alas!" it cried, as it died: "We often give our enemies the means for our own destruction."

Practical Application

Our ability to communicate effectively is one our most important resource.

Case Study

David was asked to facilitate a work group with department directors to develop a management training program. The objective was to design and implement a way to identify employees who had management potential and design a management training program that would give them sufficient skills to apply for future management positions.

David was chosen for this task because of his past experience with a similar initiative at his former job. Five other managers who had strong management profiles were selected by senior management to be part of the work group. At the first meeting David summarized senior management's expectations and outlined the parameters for designing and implementing this important new program. He also said senior management is willing to provide the resources that may be needed.

Although he had previous experience working with similar initiatives, he was not able to express his ideas very clearly on how to proceed. He tended to ramble and mix priorities when explaining his own vision of the end product, and sometimes he seemed to completely miss interpret questions from the group. The second meeting ended with the group feeling their time may be wasted with Dave working as the group's facilitator. Word got back to senior management and after the third meeting with David, a new facilitator was selected. It was clear that David's poor communication skills and lack of preparation proved to be his own feather in the arrow that ended the opportunity he had to continue.

Discussion

David's knowledge and past experience with similar services was not enough to overcome his inability to communicate effectively. This case study focuses primarily on verbal communication and listening. When thinking about our verbal communication, we tend to focus on two primary components, speaking and listening. However, effective communication requires several other important components that we sometimes don't consider seriously enough. Effective communication is as much an art as it is a process of using accepted rules and guidelines to communicate an idea. Before we talk about these various components, let's think for a moment about how much time we spend on the job, talking. It's a huge percentage of time and it's worth considering this because whenever we talk, we are creating an impression of ourselves with others. An impression that can sustain, build, or diminish how others view our credibility and competencies, and that's important because it leads others to believe, accept, or disregard our message.

Effective communication is the most basic resource we have for getting things done.

The Verbal Communication Package

Every time we say something to employees, colleagues, the boss and upper management, whom over, we create and send what I consider to be a communication package. The package includes things like tone of voice, body language, volume, style, words, and content. It also includes such things as tempo or a sense of urgency. These are important elements of our verbal communication package, and what I find interesting about this is that the absence or misuse of any one of these elements be can the most important part of the message and can lead to the listener misunderstanding the message.

Let's say there is a situation where a manager learns at the last minute that a state inspector just arrived at his facility to validate the organization's compliance with a new set of worker safety rules. The manager calls a meeting with his supervisors and says the following in a straight forward none descript manner. "I just got word a state inspector arrived to spot check our compliance with their new employee safety regulations". "You will need to be familiar with the rules and be able to show that we are compliant." The meeting ended. This delivery shows a huge gap, even a contradiction of the importance of what's happening at the facility. What does this example tell us? It tells us if the person speaking delivered a verbal communication package with missing pieces, in this case a sense of real importance and urgency it could cause the recipient of the message to miss interpret, or only partially understand the situation– and react in a different way than what the speaker intended.

A listener will have the same problem if the person talking over emphasizes the message. In this situation if the person speaking delivers a simple message with a heightened amount of urgency or enthusiasm the listeners are likely to be concerned that they have missed something in the communication and again, will be confused or react differently to what the speaker intended. These are simple examples but the point is that all the elements of our communication package need to be in balance with the situation and the speaker's central message to be fully effective.

We sometimes take for granted how the listener is interpreting our verbal message. We should consider for a moment that words, on their own, may not be the most meaningful part of the message we are trying to communicate. They are one element of their communication package, and sometimes the words are actually the least important. When we speak, we create a kind of mental image with the listener that "hooks" their thinking to the main point of the message. I can recall interactions when I could not remember exactly what someone said, but I got the message from other pieces of the communication package. Perhaps it was a particular expression on their face, or it was the way they folded their arms. It might have been how the person looked at me with an expression of confidence or with not so much confidence. Each one of these gestures could send a message that's dominates the words that were used. All elements of the communication package need to be in synch with the words that were used and the central message.

Delivering A Simple Focused Message

Efficiency when speaking is also something to consider. Efficiency in this case means using the fewest words possible and stringing them into logical phrases that will be easy to understand. A very effective way to disengage listeners is to use too many words that aren't sufficiently focused on the issue and then putting those words into "cumbersome" phrases.

There are thousands of examples when words were carefully selected to create a strong image that hooked us to the core message. President Roosevelt for example, talking about Pear Harbor, used the simple phrase "A day of infamy" to create an otherwise indescribable event to build a unanimous image with the US population about the significance of the attack. Those few carefully chosen words also created a sense of common will and bond among the people to fight back with everything we had. A detailed explanation of what happened would have been much less effective. Another quick example of efficiency in speech is when Winston Churchill talked during a radio message saying "Never in the history of humanity have so many been so grateful to so few." This simple statement created a clear understanding to his people of how so many of them were saved by the brave action of a very few courageous soldiers. These are among so many other examples that show how the use of simple well-chosen words can help listeners interpret and reduce complex scenarios into a simple central message– and how they can uniformly plant that message in all of our mines. We hear the common expression from time to time, less is more, and this can apply equally when we speak. Most of us are not likely to be called upon to deliver such weighty messages, but there will be times when we have to navigate [verbally] a difficult message through a sticky or difficult situation. That's when it's important to consider all the elements of our communication package, and have them in proper proportion to each other.

Below are four key benefits of practicing effective verbal communication techniques.

- Improves Understanding
  - Creates less opportunity for confusion and limits the opportunity for others to editorialize, improvise, or misinterpret the message.
- Improves Cooperation
  - People are more likely to provide their support if they understand the concept and the key points of the message
- Helps to Establish a measure of confidence with the audience
  - A clearly stated, accurate, and appropriately delivered

message helps to build confidence in the speaker and in the message.

- Build Efficiencies into the Delivery
  - Have the central message clearly in mind and without unnecessary explanation or clarifications.

Body Language

Our body language can telegraph what we are feeling as we speak. If the purpose of the communication is to motivate and create energy in the room, the speaker's posture should represent a certain sense of enthusiasm and confidence. If the purpose of the communication is about a more serious message the speaker's posture should be calibrated to that situation. Using appropriate body language helps the audience interpret the message more clearly.

Here are a few additional points for effective verbal communication from Todd Smith – communication consultant.

- Try to create a mental attitude that best fits the situation without pre judging a particular person or group of listeners willingness to listen or accept the message.
- Use the available space wisely. Be conscious of your proximity to the audience.
  - In a small meeting room, if standing stay in a confined area and at an appropriate distance from those listening.
  - In a large lecture hall feel free to walk about in the speaker's area
- While speaking try to make eye contact occasionally with people around the room
- Don't take the listener for granted. I have been surprised more than once when a listener reacted completely differently later to what I intended.

Todd Smith[1] a consultant on the topic of communication offers online 10 important communication skills that summarize very nicely the importance and art of effective verbal communication.

---

[1] Verbal Communication Skills Worth Mastering/ little things matter http:// littlethingsmatter.com/blog

- Be friendly
  - o We are subconsciously drawn to people who are friendly because they make us feel good and bring more enjoyment to our lives.
- Think Before You Speak
  - o Many people say whatever goes into their minds without putting a thought into what they are saying.... which ends up reflecting poorly on themselves.
- Be Clear
  - o Most of us don't have the time nor do we want to spend our emotional energy to figure out what someone else is trying to way. When there is something you want to say, ask yourself, what is the best way I can communicate the point....
- Don't Talk Too Much
  - o Very few people like to be around someone who talks to much and dominates the conversation.
- Be Your Authentic Self
  - o People are attracted to someone who speaks from the heart and is genuine, transparent, and real.
- Practice Humility
  - o Humility is having a modest view of one's own importance. People who speak with humility and genuine respect for others are almost always held in high regard.
- Speak with Confidence
  - o Speaking with confidence does not counter the need for humility. Speaking with confidence includes words you choose, the tone of your voice, your eye contact, and body language. These are supported by what you have validated and know to be correct.
- Focus on Body Language
  - o Body language communicates respect and interest in those listening. It gives real meaning to your words.
- Be Concise
  - o We become irritated when someone speaking can't get

to the point. As yourself, how can I say what needs to be said in the fewest words possible while being courteous and respectful.

- Learn the Art of Listening
  - Being an attentive listener is as important in verbal communications than any words that can come out of your mouth. Show sincere interest in what is being said, ask good questions, listen for the message within the message, and avoid interrupting.

Brain First–Mouth Second

Hopefully when communicating, the mouth is driven by the brain and not the other way around. As you may have heard or read, each side of the brain carries out a fairly specific set of functions. Although more recent research shows the left-right brain functions are not as specific as we once thought, still we all have the ability to think logically and analytically. It helps us avoid being tricked or fooled. We can also think in a more analog and abstract way which helps us to interpret situations, imagine, and be creative. These are extremely narrow descriptions but they begin to show us how they apply to making good verbal communication.

Let's consider athletes for a moment. We have heard sports commentators describe an athlete before, let's say making a ski run. The athlete is preparing with eyes closed and using their brain to visualize all the turns they will encounter while skiing down a mountain side. Doing this helps them anticipate and navigate each turn because once on the run, there's no time to think in detail about the moves they need to make. Once on their run they are functioning in a mental zone that they created before-hand. A gymnast will pause, concentrate, and perform their routine mentally in the same way.

These exercises are an essential preparation regimen so they can manage what's about to happen. Such an intense level of mental preparation probably won't be necessary with our day-to-day communications, but it does encourage us to think about and even practice preparing for what we want to say. Even in the most casual situations we should be aware of self before speaking and take a moment to consider all the elements we plan in our communication package. Doing so will help us deliver difficult messages more effectively and it helps others be more confident and willing to accept what we say.

The Art of Listening

What…. What did she say????

Listening also requires a huge percentage of our time, and what we [hear] helps us understand what was said and how that message can be interpreted. Unfortunately, humans are not great listeners and there are many reasons for this. I remember a classroom exercise. A very short message was given to the first person in a classroom of about 15 young adults. By the time that sentence reached and was interpreted by the 15th person, it could hardly be recognized.

As adults, we deal with many distractions and urgencies that can lead us to [hear] something that's different from what was said. Here's a simple analogy. I happened to be listening to a CD that was playing through a CD player. The CD had a few flawed areas that caused the player to skip so nothing could be heard for a fraction of a second. But when I played the same CD through my computer, the music sounded fine. The difference was the computer had the ability to average "stitch" electronically the flawed areas on a disc together so what I heard through the computer seemed fine. We can do the same kind of stitching with the "computers" on our shoulders. Our mind can actually fill the gaps when we are distracted for a second and "tells" us what we [think] we [should] have heard or expected to hear rather than what was actually said. In other situations, our minds allow us to drift into another world altogether and day dream while we believe we are really listening. Maybe we were recalling a troublesome conversation we had recently, or it may be about sending that overdue mortgage payment tonight. All the while we believe we are listening to what was said.

Like speaking, listening seems to be an easy thing to do, but listening requires a certain awareness and certain skill as well. In fact, it's a skill that we need to practice throughout the day.

Here are just a few conditions that can minimize our ability to hear the message.

- We hear something that strikes us a certain way and we immediately move to possible arguments about what was said and in the process we lose focus on what was actually said.
- Our minds move too quickly to solving a problem that was presented and we block or miss interpret what was said
- We don't agree with the information that was presented and we get upset or angry which allows us to miss interpret or mentally turn off the speaker.
- Outside distractions may be competing with our ability to focus on the what was said
- Our minds drift to a personal issue we may be struggling with
- We consider the information boring and repetitive and mentally turn it off.

Faulty listening not only leads us to a misinterpretation, that misinterpretation can cause us to react in the wrong way to something that was said. We can sometimes mix what we thought we heard with what the speaker said. Or allow our own prejudges, beliefs, fears about the subject to override or become a part of what we [think] someone said.

For example, let's say we hear something with which we agree and are pleased. How might that message be managed? Well, we might simply agree and feel good about the message. Or we may be so enthusiastic about the message that we unwittingly assume add, infer, or interpret and stitch additional ideas of our own into what was said. The problem here is the speaker didn't actually say what the listener added so the listener may leave the conversation or the meeting thinking the speaker believes or is advocating more than he/she actually said. Sounds unlikely? How many times have we heard someone say to the listener…. no, that's not what I said. A listener's primary responsibility is not to agree or disagree, it is to hear the words being spoken and interpret them as accurately as possible without filtering in any way.

Another example of aberrant listening is when a listener hears something he or she doesn't agree with. Here, a listener may feel angry or offended with what was said and take the liberty, again Unwittingly and assume the speaker believes or is advocating a more extreme idea than what was in the actual message. We know we should be active listeners, but hearing the words alone isn't active listening. Listening carries with it the responsibility to interpret the message accurately without truncating or extending what was said.

These problems can be avoided many times by simply being more aware of these possibilities when listening and taking the time to ask the speaker for clarification. "Would you state that a little differently for me". We don't generally think in terms of managing what we say and hear, but in fact that is exactly our responsibility in both cases. When the situation doesn't allow for questions, we have no choice but to interpret what was said as accurately and objectively as possible while keeping the above discussion in mind.

When We Can't Listen

There are other times when we simply can't stop and listen or initiate a conversation correctly. However, even this simple situation needs to be managed to avoid unintended problems. When this occurs, the only thing we can do is to make a commitment to have the conversation at another time. Ask the person to phone later, "Please make an appointment to talk", or "stop into my office later". Making an offer to communicate at another time demonstrates common courtesy.

Our eyes can determine how well we are listening to the speaker. If we are looking through a window and watching how hard the wind is blowing, our eyes and minds are locked on the wind not what is being said.

Speaking and listening are huge topics that can be given much more time for discussion than what is available in this simple commonsense discussion. As was noted at the beginning of this chapter, exercising strong speaking and listening skills is essential, and developing strong communication skills can be a leader's career survival tool and one of the most important means for establishing one's ability to get things done.

Chapter Summary

When Speaking

- ➤ Using simple and effective communication techniques is a career builder.
- ➤ Some preparation is always needed even with casual conversation. This includes such things as;
  - ○ Choice of words
  - ○ Tone of voice
  - ○ Appropriate body language
  - ○ Formulating a clear central message
  - ○ Be aware of our mindset when anticipating a conversation.
    - ▪ Feeling angry, distrustful, challenged, etc. before speaking will be recognized by those listening. Beginning a conversation with these emotions can draw attention to the speaker and away from the message.
    - ▪ It can also result in an unintended follow up by the listener
  - ○ Gauge the nature of the conversation in advance and select words, tone, and manner that best fits the circumstances.
    - ▪ Consider the communication package
- ➤ Use mental imagery to visualize the central message you want to deliver and determine how it can be delivered in a convincing way
  - ○ Use simple sentences that carry logical and focused ideas
- ➤ Visualize the person or group you are talking to in the most favorable light possible.

When Listening

- ➤ Active listening is more than hearing the words, it also requires verification, focusing on the words, recognizing the central message, and interpreting the message correctly.
  - ○ Sometimes the listener needs to be "brave" and take the

opportunity to ask follow up questions.

- o Separate the person speaking from what is being said. A speaker's mannerisms and mode of speaking can sometimes be distracting, misleading, or frustrating to a listener.
- ➢ Be aware that what you are thinking is where your eyes are focused.
- ➢ When circumstances do not allow for an immediate conversation, provide an opportunity to have the discussion at another time.
- ➢ Verbal communication [speaking and listening] requires simple but important techniques that need to be practiced.
- ➢ Good communications skills are career building skills

CHAPTER FIVE

MANAGING MULTIPLE PROJECTS

The Boy and the Filberts

A boy put his hand into a pitcher full of filberts. He grasped as many as he could possibly hold, but when he tried to pull out his hand, he was prevented from doing so by the neck of the pitcher. Unwilling to lose his filberts, and yet unable to withdraw his hand, he burst into tears and bitterly lamented his disappointment. A bystander said to him, "Be satisfied with half the quantity, and you will readily draw out your hand."

Do not attempt too much at once

Practical Application

Even the most difficult personnel or operations problems can be address successfully by using a simple regimen to identify its most basic components and causes.

Case Study

Jeff was happy to be promoted to director of a busy high-profile division with over 500 employees but he knew this promotion comes with challenges. He quickly began to see just how many employee and operations challenges there were when he chaired his first operations meeting with his 10 managers. He also began to see his managers were frustrated with their efforts to make improvements and manage their employees. There were customer service complaints, and four of his inherited departments had serious budget issues. In addition, the union seemed to be doing everything possible to encourage conflict between employees and their managers. Jeff also knew their employees had been complaining loudly to senior management. Jeff knew these problems were long standing issues which now reached a critical point where senior management was anxious to have them resolved.

Discussion

In this case study, Jeff had a wide range of problems to solve so he had to be clear about his first steps toward finding solutions. Like the boy who tried to grab too many filberts at the same time and got stuck, Jeff had to resist the temptation and the pressure he was feeling to solve too many of these problems at the same time and too quickly. The central message here is to not shoot first and ask questions later despite the temptation to show progress. Jeff's first step is to take no action and instead gather information. He must begin a thorough assessment of the situation, interpret the information accurately, set priorities, and then think about action plans. Trying to shoot "alligators" in the pond before developing a solid plan only creates a temporary void that others alligators will be happy to fill.

But how can he get the reliable information he needs and buy time with the boss? He must first use his communication skills to explain his approach to his boss. He needs to schedule one on one discussions with his managers about the current issues so he can begin to separate symptoms from anecdotes to understand what's actually happening. He also needs to get more detailed feedback directly from department supervisors who are closer to what's happening on the floor, and finally talk with employees at their staff meetings.

Jeff also needs to know if everyone is seeing the problems in the same way because it's virtually impossible to implement solutions when people are seeing and interpreting the same situation differently. These gaps in understanding will almost always lead those involved to advocate different action plans. He must work to get everyone to see cause and effect in the same way and that requires strong communication skills, time, and an ability to make accurate assessments convincingly.

The likelihood of Jeff being able to buy time to solve these problems increases substantially if he can clearly articulate the situation to his boss with sufficient details that he can validate. He needs to convince his boss that he is doing his homework so his boss will be willing to support him with resources and time.

Check List for Evaluating the Situation
- Separate symptoms from root cause
- Assess the leadership skills of his managers and supervisors
- Know which resources he will need
   - Are outside resources needed, HR, IT, available to help
- Understand the cultural and core values of the workplace environment
   - Assess how easily the current workplace environment will accept new action plans
- Take action when possible in order to show evidence of progress
- Be able to visualize the various pieces of the puzzle clearly and understand how they fit into the current scenario
- Have a clear idea of how progress can be measured.
- Know the key upper management people who may be watching
   - How will they measure or evaluate his progress?
   - Be sure to have their support before taking action

As the new division manager, Jeff has to know if he can depend on his managers and supervisors to implement new ideas and action plans properly. Will they take direction easily. Are they sufficiently committed to do what's necessary? Are they mentally strong enough to address the push back that may come from employees. Before taking action, Jeff needs to be sure his managers and supervisors are going to be part of the solution and not part of the problem. He will be depending on their mental strength and commitment to do what is necessary. How closely will he have to work with each manager, and how closely will his manager's need to work with their supervisors in order to achieve the desired outcome. The only way he can get answers to these questions is by having open and frank conversations with his managers and supervisors. He knows he, must at the same time, be willing to accept and work with his untrained managers when they make errors in judgement and be ready to provide coaching when indicated.

He also needs to get employee feedback on what they are experiencing. I remember a conversation I had with a very successful venture capitalist. These are people who buy failing or sometimes small start-up businesses and turn them into more profitable operations. I asked what he contributes to his successes in turning the businesses he buys into successful ventures. Does he get much information from the organizations' leaders and his answer was surprising. He said, actually he spends more time touring the individual departments talking with employees about what they see is happening and listens carefully to their observations and comments. He said they experience the operation's inconsistencies and obstacles that upper management sometimes pay little attention to. The effect of those accumulated factors can be substantial.

Only after Jeff has all the information he needs to understand the situation fully, can he ask his boss to make an investment of time and resources that may be needed. Jeff also needs to show his commitment and confidence.

There are various tools that can help Jeff and his managers visualize and understand what brought them to their current condition. But open, frank, and respectful discussions with his managers and employees will be a crucial resource. He must be able to separate facts from personal opinion, guess work, and fabrication.

While having these discussions, Jeff should also be sensitive to what has not been said. Not hearing certain comments, descriptions, or phrases can be telling. Getting what feels like one word or truncated answers may indicate something is being shielded, or overlooked. Jeff needs to be aware that his employees, managers, and supervisors may not always be comfortable discussing situations to the fullest, so he must be able to "read between the lines". It's always worthwhile to ask different people the same question and evaluate their comments carefully. People who work in a positive environment are willing to offer comments and clarifications freely and that will always feel better then when someone is holding back. We can only rely on our instincts when sensing something is missing or doesn't feel quite right.

The main thing we can do with these conversations is to create, as much as possible, a sense among all involved of safety and confidentiality and a clear understanding of the facts.

Time Needed for Fact Finding

Of course, the amount of time that's needed to make a thorough assessment varies. It may seem that the above regimen requires a lot of time, too much perhaps while the boss and upper management are looking for results. It may also seem to be too regimented. However, each of the steps described will provide essential details that can lead to a targeted and accurate assessment of a complicated situation that could have many moving parts and extending situations that he may not be aware of. Jeff also had to learn how to work with the key people in HR and with union representatives. In this case study, Jeff was able to provide a sufficiently clear action plan to his boss in a little more than 6 weeks while being able to make small improvements along the way.

His ability to distinguish between root cause, symptoms, and anecdotes saved a lot of time and helped him build credibility with his managers and employees. That could only have happened with the process described above. He was able to use his intellect and apply simple commonsense to clarify a confusing situation. His consideration of human nature's expectations helped him navigate successfully through a maze of personnel circumstances. He also exercised the wisdom he gained from his past management experiences which gave him the confidence he needed to anticipate what would or would not work under the current circumstances. He was also able to create a no-fault environment when he talked with others about specific circumstances. And finally, he was able to support his managers while providing strong direction.

Managing Antagonists

The tone and progress we feel during a fact-finding meeting with employees can be dominated by one or a few who make it difficult to discuss issues objectively. Antagonists who make aggressive or passive aggressive comments or accusations only disrupt the flow of worthwhile discussions. Facilitators need to watch for this and address it promptly and directly. One strategy is to ignore the antagonist by redirecting the discussions to other members rather than spending time on their comments or anecdotes. But sometimes that strategy doesn't work and in those instances the group leader needs to take a dominant posture and address the person directly by telling them their comments are being disruptive and counter-productive. In more extreme situations, it may be necessary to address the situation in a more direct manner privately.

More than Great Ideas

Finally, Jeff needs to be sure his action plans have the proper underpinning. For example, developing a new set of procedures to improve the efficiency of a service or quality of a product would be useless if employee competencies, equipment, or financial resources weren't sufficient to sustain the initiative. Great ideas need to be accompanied with the right amount of [under pinning] to create the best opportunity for success. These examples may seem obvious and very basic, yet it's surprising how often well-developed action plans and initiatives have fallen short because a critical piece was overlooked.

Chapter Summary

- ➤ Resist the temptation to tackle too many issues at the same time.
  - ○ Get suggestions from department managers, supervisors, and line employees about what can be addressed sooner rather than later.
  - ○ Determine which problems [if any] can be packaged and addressed at the same time.
- ➤ Get the key people involved to understand and agree on the cause and effect of each issue
  - ○ There must be agreement among managers, supervisors on how department issues are to be addressed.
- ➤ Having open discussions with employees at meetings is helpful when fact finding.
- ➤ Be clear about the sequence for implementing action plans.
- ➤ Be clear about the resources [underpinning] that may be needed to support the action plan
  - ○ Make sure provisions for training, new policies and procedures, etc. are in place before the plan is implemented.
- ➤ Research best practices and consider how they can be incorporated into the action plan.
- ➤ Be able to visualize how each element of the action plan will affect the problem [s] you want to solve.
- ➤ Establish specific indicators that can be used to mark progress and successes and be clear about how progress will be measured.
- ➤ Set realistic timelines.
- ➤ Create an environment for safe communication when talking about problems with management personnel and employees.
- ➤ Be willing to take advice and make adjustments to the action plan where indicated.
- ➤ Manage antagonists
- ➤ Mastery of the details helps assure a successful outcome.
  - ○ Avoid the temptation to act on assumptions. Sometimes what seems obvious needs to be double checked and validated before taking action.

CHAPTER SIX

RECOGNIZING AND MANAGING WORK-AROUNDS

The Mountains in Labour

One day the Countrymen noticed that the Mountains were in labour; smoke came out of their summits, the earth was quaking at their feet, trees were crashing, and huge rocks were tumbling. They felt sure that something horrible was going to happen. They all gathered together in one place to see what terrible thing this could be. They waited and they waited, but nothing came. At last there was a still more violent earthquake, and a huge gap appeared in the side of the Mountains. They all fell down upon their knees and waited. At last, and at last, a teeny, tiny mouse poked its little head and bristles out of the gap and came running down towards them, and ever after they used to say:

Much outcry, little outcome.

Practical Application

Avoid using interim or work around fixes.

Case Study

Sam manages a service that performs complex medical procedures which are accomplished in an OR setting. These procedures can require up to four hours to complete. The physicians who perform these services are recognized by the hospital's medical staff as being highly skilled. They also enjoy national recognition for using cutting-edge techniques, the articles they published in major medical journals, and the lectures they present nationally.

A talented support staff of technologists and nurses work with the physicians to perform these vascular interventional (repair) procedures throughout the body including the brain. The technologists report to a technical manager and the nurses report to a licensed acute-care nurse who coordinates operations with the technical manager.

Despite the competencies and the recognition they all enjoy, there are long-standing simmering issues in the workplace that too often cause confusion, frustration, and delays throughout the day. The frustration comes mostly from simple miss communications between the three work groups, not having immediate access to equipment and supplies during a procedure, and fitting emergent add-on cases into their already full schedule. Also, the department's operating expenses are over budget.

Physicians view the patient-care competencies of the nurses and the technical staff as being very satisfactory, but they point to their supervisor's poor operations management skills as the reason for the dysfunction. However, both the nurses and technologists view the physicians as being the main problem and point to the physicians' unwillingness to follow guidelines and rules when approving and scheduling cases and not being available to start cases on time. Despite low morale among the technologists and nurses, turnover has been virtually zero.

Sam conducted a few meetings with the technologists and nurses to sort out their complaints and find ways to resolve their operations issues. The lead physician would occasionally attend these meetings, but no matter how well the discussions seemed to progress, things continued with virtually no improvement.

Despite these simmering internal problems, physicians and their patients view the quality of the medical work they accomplished as exceptional. Often, extraordinary efforts are needed to create space in the day's already full schedule to accommodate an urgent add-on case. In fact, emergency add-on cases are common. Ironically it is during these adverse and high-pressure situations when everyone finds a way to pull together, and almost instinctively perform the procedure with a high level of efficiency. It is also when everyone feels an especially strong sense of professional pride in each other's work– and further, it seems these circumstances is what sustains their willingness to stay. Their pride in the life-saving work they do and their dedication encourages them to make compromises and stay with it and not leave.

Discussion

Here's a situation where we have three work groups with highly talented and dedicated people who continue to perform complex lifesaving medical procedures under extremely frustrating circumstances. Yet, after several process improvement sessions they could not come together and find ways to improve operations. In fact, it seems that rather than trying to understand cause an effect, they continued to fill their time at their meetings with anecdotes that served only to defect their own accountability to their coworkers. As a result, work continued each day by using work-arounds as a "fix" and unwittingly tricking themselves into thinking those work-arounds were part of the solution. In fact, some of their workarounds seemed to work so well that they provided a kind of rationale to continue.

As was noted earlier work arounds, no matter how well they may seem to be compensating for real solutions only encourage these simmering "Mountains in Labour" scenarios to continue. One of the major concerns is doing this can play into a perfect storm scenario with tragic results. We have read about these scenarios in newspapers with various industries, from airlines, automobile, etc. when the reluctance or inability to [fix] a known problem led to a catastrophic outcome. Fortunately, no such circumstance occurred with this case study.

Getting Everyone Together

One of the problems in this case study is that the medical director did not have total authority to manage the physicians in his group and it was the physicians who screened and approved the cases. After their approval, it was up to the nurse manager to find a way to fit the cases into the schedule. Also, the medical director's rotating schedule made it difficult to attend all the process improvement meetings. E-mail communications were used to keep everyone aware of what was discussed at the meetings but that was not a good substitute for his absence and input. Sam's boss had been following these meetings and decided to send an email to the two managers and medical director that summarized his understanding of the situation. The email noted the lack of commitment to resolve these issues – stopped the meetings and asked the lead technologist and nurse to draft a set of clearly defined expectations for scheduling cases, equipment and supplies availability, and a procedure for approving cases. The email also called for an end to using anecdotes and accusations for the purpose of shunting responsibility, and reminded everyone that having meetings is not taking action.

Best Practice

Obviously, there needs to be much more than having a set of newly defined expectations and commitments. The two supervisors had no formal training in operations management. They had been learning this new skill on the job so they decided to visit a few facilities where similar procedures were performed. They also studied journal articles and after a short time came across two journal articles that were very helpful in describing best practices.

After a few weeks of working with the information they began to find ways to apply what they learned to the current situation, and began to work with Sam's boss to finalize the draft. The new operations procedures included such things as how cases are to be scheduled, who could approve add-on cases, a new system for ordering and keeping supplies in the procedure rooms along with several other operational refinements. The new operations plan was given a one-month evaluation. After that time a follow up meeting was scheduled to review progress. During the evaluation period the service functioned more efficiently and they decided to continue while making a few minor adjustments.

The point here is progress was possible only after they were able to sort out the work-arounds and see specific cause and effect, make commitments to comply, and each group take responsibility for their part of the process.

Chapter Summary

- ➢ List, clarify, and get agreement on each of the operations and personnel issues.
- ➢ Use various tools that are available to identify processes and root cause.
- ➢ Show how each problem impacts operating efficiencies, costs, wasted supplies, and employee morale.
- ➢ Be clear about the need for support processes [underpinning].
    - ○ Availability of equipment, supplies, efficient paper work procedures, and inventory control are common problems.
    - ○ Provide additional training if indicated
- ➢ Be clear about the specific issues that need to be "fixed"
- ➢ Having meeting [s] should not be thought of as– taking action.
- ➢ Set specific performance standards and expectations, and institute clearly defined action for noncompliance.
- ➢ Research Best Practice and build as many best practice elements into the final operations plan as possible.

CHAPTER SEVEN

MANAGING EMPLOYEE ERRORS

The Young Thief and His Mother

A young Man had been caught in a daring act of theft and had been condemned to be executed for it. He expressed his desire to see his Mother, and to speak with her before he was led to execution, and of course this was granted. When his Mother came to him he said: "I want to whisper to you," and when she brought her ear near him, he nearly bit it off. All the bystanders were horrified, and asked him what he could mean by such brutal and inhuman conduct. "It is to punish

her," he said. "When I was young I began with stealing little things, and brought them home to Mother. Instead of rebuking and punishing me, she laughed and said: "It will not be noticed." It is because of her that I am here to-day."

"He is right, woman," said the Priest; "the Lord hath said:

'Train up a child in the way he should go; and when he is old he will not depart therefrom.'"

Practical Application

A central responsibility of a leader is to provide strong direction, train, mentor, and coach.

Case Study

Sally managed a department that had been getting upsetting feedback about the quality of service her department provides and learned that some of her employees had growing concerns as well about errors their coworkers were making. She also learned a few of her employees had been complaining about being "picked on" when her supervisors approached them about the errors they were making. The situation eventually reached a point where Sally had to do something about the quality of work and the bickering.

Sally's department provides a wide range of highly specialized medical imaging services. All of her employees graduated from certified schools but the technology and complexity of procedures her department perform seems to advance almost by the month. Sally and her supervisors knew something had to be done beyond their pleas for employees to be more careful. As Sally and her supervisors researched the problem, they became even more confused because some of the errors were made consistently by their most experienced and knowledgeable people.

Discussion

Sally's employees make complex entries on a computer driven console while a procedure is in progress which can require up to 50 minutes of concentrated work. Sally and her supervisors worked with their employees in various ways to minimize the errors but the errors continued. She began to feel her employees were just being careless and decided to use progressive discipline, but it had no impact on the frequency or type of errors. It only created more tension in the workplace.

The atmosphere became contentious and Sally called for assistance from the HR department. A trained facilitator, Jonathan was asked to help Sally get to the bottom of the problem and find solutions. Sally gave Jonathan an initial briefing and he scheduled a meeting with Sally's employees. She thought the value of having an "outside" person facilitating these meetings could help create a better atmosphere for open discussion and possibly greater objectivity and understanding. It became clear during their first meeting that the employees were as upset about the errors as Sally. Sally listened and held back on participating. She knew there would be time later for clarification with Jonathan.

Sally's employees identified the following during the meeting:

- Employees are expected to make critical settings on a control panel during lengthy procedures.
- The control panels are located in a busy work area.
- The procedures require highly skilled technologists
- Each test requires its own regimen of complex settings at the control panel
- Their service provides a wide range of tests from simple 10 minute procedures to the more difficult and complex studies

The employee's meeting with Jonathan also gave Sally an opportunity to hear her employee's concerns in a slightly different way than if she had been the facilitator. Jonathan and Sally knew all of the employees' complaints may not be entirely valid, but for the moment, the primary objective was to get the employees to vent about what they thought was happening and hear all there was to hear. The realities could be worked out later. Sally knew all of her employees had proper certifications from reputable schools, but began to wonder if that by itself is enough to guarantee their ability to perform all of their procedures, and started to wonder what other factors may be contributing to the problem.

Sally met with her supervisors to discuss their employees' feedback and took a careful look at the procedures they perform. They soon began to realize the variances of complexity among the procedures is huge. After more thought they were able to organize all the procedures into categories of difficulty and were able to identify five distinct levels. Their employee onboarding procedure was packaged into one general orientation session with the assumption that their newly hired employees' certifications provided sufficient grounding so all they needed was on-the-job training.

Then Sally and her supervisors reviewed the errors from the past six months and identified the employees who performed the errors, and decided to talk with them individually. The interviews were conducted in a relaxed manner with a clear emphasis on the need to understand any contributing factor [s] that may be involved. This fact-finding process was acknowledged by the employees and was completed in two weeks. The interviews also helped Sally and her supervisors realize discipline was not the answer and [in effect] let their employees "out of "error jail".

Also, these fact-finding sessions began to shed light on one the most confusing things which was why so many errors were consistently made by Sally's competent and conscientious employees. The employees talked about this indirectly during their meeting with Jonathan.

The control panels are located in a relatively small work area where there could be as many as three other coworkers talking and performing other tasks. The work area also served as the department's central observation area and it became clear how distracting that scenario could be to anyone working at the two consoles. Unfortunately, there was no other space available for employees to perform those other tasks. With this Sally began to understand how some employees could be distracted by the peripheral activity and simply lose focus while working at the console, and could see how having the required technical skills alone may not be sufficient to perform all 5 level of procedures. Her employees must be able to ignore the distractions and stay focused on the machine. She also realized no amount of certification, training, or discipline could build that important trait into her employees.

Action Steps

With the information they gathered, Sally began to visualize an action plan. First, she understood a new training regimen was needed which had to be aligned with the five specific competencies that are needed for each of the procedure categories. Second, the procedure manuals they were using hand-written sometimes hard to read notations instead of typed updates. Third, additional copies of procedure books needed to be placed in more convenient locations to allow for easy access. Four, all future entries in the procedure books must be approved and entered by supervisors. Previously, many had been written by employees after getting word of mouth instructions from physicians. And five, Sally had to think about the workplace environment, but knew there was no other space that could be used to separate the general activity from the consoles. And finally, she had to find a way to deal with the employees who might not be able to work in that high energy and distracting environment. In addition to all of that, her action plan had to be supported by the employees' union.

It turned out that four employees were involved with the errors. There were two long term employees and two others had less time on the job. Sally talked with each employee separately and told them she could not allow the errors to continue, and that she believed the errors are not related to their competencies or their work ethic. Sally said she felt the errors were the result of losing focus in the current distracting environment. She also said she believed additional training would not help.

After thinking and talking about possible solutions with Jonathan, Sally decided to have the four employees consider three options. One was to fill two vacancies she had at another location in the same health system that performed the same studies but in a much more controlled environment. Second, continue to work and if the errors continued be subject to disciplinary action and possible dismissal. Three, resign and seek employment elsewhere. With this option, Sally would provide strong references knowing their skills and appreciating the current working conditions are difficult. She would allow them to continue for a reasonable amount of time so they could find a similar position at one of the facilities in the community. She knew they would have no difficulty finding a job in one of the surrounding facilities. Given these options, the two long term employees decided to fill the vacancies Sally had elsewhere in the system. The remaining two employees decided to accept the resignation option Sally made.

The next step for Sally was to design a new and more formal training program for all five procedure levels. Here is a summary of their new training plan.

1. Each employee had to pass a written test and had to perform a procedure that was in each level of difficulty while being observed by a supervisor. If they passed the test and were able to demonstrate their proficiency while performing all of the procedures, a statement of competence would be placed in the employee's personnel file.

   ○ Employees who were not able to demonstrate their competency were permitted to select a supervisor or coworker who was approved by a supervisor to get additional on-the-job training.
   ○ If the schedule allowed, they could work with their trainer during normally scheduled work hours. They were also granted a fixed amount of overtime pay to come during [none shift] hours to get their additional training.
   ○ Employees had to complete their additional training in a given time period in order to receive a department competence letter without fear of disciplinary action.
   ○ Employees who were getting additional training could perform only the less complex procedures until they received their department competency letter.

Sally's supervisors edited and re-wrote the procedure manuals. All new employees had to go through the same screening process so they could receive a [department certification] and become qualified to perform all of the procedures the department offered.

As the fable and case study show, defaulting to discipline without accounting for contributing factors can create additional problems for managers. In fact, there is almost never only one cause with these types of problems. Managers should not assume formal certifications alone are sufficient to assure an employee's competency and ability to perform, which meant Sally and her supervisors also had to evaluate their screening, interviewing, hiring, and on-boarding practices.

CHAPTER EIGHT

PLANNING FOR OPERATIONS IMPROVEMENTS

Belling the Cat

Long ago, the mice had a general council to consider what measures they could take to outwit their common enemy, the Cat. Some said this, and some said that; but at last a young mouse got up and said he had a proposal to make, which he thought would meet the case. "You will all agree," said he, "that our chief danger consists in the sly and treacherous manner in which the enemy approaches us. Now, if we could receive some signal of her approach, we could easily escape

from her. I venture, therefore, to propose that a small bell be procured, and attached by a ribbon round the neck of the Cat. By this means we should always know when she was about, and could easily retire while she was in the neighborhood."

This proposal met with general applause, until an old mouse got up and said:

"That is all very well, but who is to bell the Cat?" The mice looked at one another and nobody spoke. Then the old mouse said:

"It is easy to propose impossible remedies."

Practical Application

We should not let the enthusiasm and confidence we may have for a solution to out weight the need to consider all the stakeholders and support open communication with all who may be affected.

Case Study

Howard was asked to manage the hospital's inpatient transportation service in addition to his current responsibilities. The service performs high volume patient transports throughout a large hospital and was experiencing a growing number of complaints about the unpredictability of patient pickup and deliveries to and from nursing floors and various diagnostic areas. Howard was asked to establish new patient scheduling transport procedures that would lead to a more reliable service.

Howard decided to create a workgroup of department heads and nurses who were experiencing these problems and called a meeting so they could talk through their experiences and work toward an action plan. After the fifth meeting everyone felt they had a good handle on the problem and had gained an understanding of how the current issues could be solved. They also knew the transporters were experienced, hard workers, and they would be eager to work with a new operations plan.

The workgroup asked their IT department to find a computer application they could use to schedule patient pickups and deliveries. They also drafted new procedures for requesting and scheduling patient pickup and deliveries. And, an additional software application was requested to allow for real time communication between the nursing floors, diagnostic centers, the transporters, and their dispatcher. It was an expensive solution but essential for creating a reliable and efficient patient transportation system. Almost 2,000 pickups and deliveries were made throughout the hospital each day. The scheduling system could also track transporters progress while on route with patients so all users could monitor in their areas what was happening real-time throughout the hospital. Having this information also allowed the transporter's dispatcher to better coordinate urgent procedures and keep everyone informed. Everyone was enthusiastic and confident their new plan would be successful.

An announcement was sent to all nursing floors and the diagnostic testing areas that the new scheduling and communications system would be implemented after training for all users was completed. The first day of operations indicated some hope for its success, but by the third day, the new plan was not showing the expected results, and actually produced additional problems. In fact, the implementation proved to be a disaster, and the money spent was being questioned by senior management.

Discussion

As we see in the fable *Belling the Cat*, the work group's great ideas alone were not enough to solve their patient transport problems. Their great sounding ideas, assumptions, and obvious solutions were not researched thoroughly enough. The work group scheduled an emergency meeting to find out what went wrong. After a short time, they began to realize the workgroup never talked with the transporters. The transporters had not been consulted or invited to participate in the planning meetings because Howard and the others assumed their own [user] experiences provided all the information they needed to move ahead. The group's members felt confident they knew all the details of the problem so the solutions were based solely on their own first-hand observations and experiences.

The problem, of course, was they didn't know– what they didn't know and they let their confidence and enthusiasm for their great ideas overlook the possibility that there may be broader issues to consider. They didn't take in account the possible underlying issues their transporters had to deal with. They simply felt too comfortable with their great sounding ideas. They scheduled a follow up meeting with three transporters and began to hear about those [other] issues. The transporters discussed in detail the world they live in which is very different from what the work group had assumed.

- Transporters spent approximately 25 percent of their time looking for wheelchairs and litters– not transporting.
- An estimated 15 percent of wheelchairs and litters were not usable because they were dirty, broken, or didn't have needed accessories.
- The current transporters' schedule did not give the nurses on patient floors or the various diagnostic departments adequate notice of a patient pickup– so patients were often not ready to leave. This meant transporters spent a lot of time standing around waiting for patients to be changed and prepared for their trip.
- Patient transport delays sometimes caused procedures to be rescheduled for another day which increased patients' length of stay in the hospital.
- Nurses on the floor were sometimes not able to administrator exam preps in sufficient time for pickup which also resulted in waisted time and tests being rescheduled.
- Despite their time on the job, transporters needed additional training in;
  - Handling emergent-patient situations while on route
  - Basic language training so they could communicate better with patients.
  - Transporters also needed additional in-service training on body mechanics to help reduce their physical strain while lifting and moving patients.

- A few transporters were on medical leave because of back sprains or other on the job injuries.

The group soon began to see why their initial plan failed and they started to work on a new operations plan.

- A designated central area was identified in the facility to store enough wheelchairs and litters.
- A maintenance person was assigned to make timely repairs on broken wheelchairs and litters.
- The new digital communication and transporter tracking system needed to be tweaked.
- The physical therapy department was asked to create a body mechanics training program to help transporters move patients and prevent injury.
- A more detailed description of the program and a new implementation plan was written and sent to all clinical areas of the hospital.
- Monitoring tools were built into their procedures to help measure the success of the revised program.

Being broad minded enough to invite all the possible stake holders to discuss a project and fact find is the only way to achieve the best possible outcome no matter how uncomfortable, unnecessary, or time consuming it may seem. The work group's enthusiasm and their self-imposed urgency to implement a new plan only worked to narrow the scope of their ability to fact find. Howard also realized that he avoided inviting people because [he] didn't want someone else "tampering" with what was surely a brilliant plan and felt doing so could only create unnecessary complications.

Chapter Summary

When Planning for a Change in Operations.

- ➤ Make a list of key personnel in the organization who may be realistically affected by the final plan and invite them to represent all those who may be affected.
- ➤ Document the key elements of the problem that need to be improved and don't lose sight of them throughout the process.
    - O Be sure these elements are adequately addressed in the action plan
- ➤ Invite those who will be primarily impacted by the plan to critique the action plan early enough in the process to allow for adjustments.
    - O Be sure all the stake holder's issues are accounted for in the final plan.
    - O Be sure the expectations of support and cooperation from other areas can be validated.
    - O Consider and secure all the underpinning items that may be needed to support and maintain the plan are accounted for.
- ➤ Define how the outcome will be assessed.
    - O Determine what monitoring tools will be used to measure progress and success.
    - O Determine who will use these tools and how information will be communicated to the project manager.
- ➤ Make sure all those who will be responsible for implementing the plan are adequately trained and capable.
- ➤ Celebrate milestones reached during planning and implementation.

CHAPTER NINE

IMPLEMENTING AND MANAGING CHANGE

The Fox and Goat

Once a fox was roaming in the dark. As ill luck would have it, he fell into a well. He tried his best to come out but all to no use. So, he had to remain there till the next morning.

At about fore-noon the next day, a goat came that way. She peeped into the well and saw the fox there.

"What are you doing there, Mr. Fox?" asked the goat.

"I came here to drink water. It is the best I have ever tasted. Come and see for yourself," replied the sly fox.

Without thinking even a bit, the goat jumped into the well. She quenched her thirst and looked for a way to get out.

The fox said, "I've an idea. Stand on your hind legs. I'll climb on your head and get out. Then I shall help you out too." The silly goat did so and the fox got out of the well.

While walking away, he said,"Had you have half as many brains as horns you would never got in without seeing how to get out."

Look before you leap

Practical Application

Leaders often want to initiate change in their organizations but sometimes don't account for one the most important pieces of the puzzle, human nature's most basic expectations.

Case Study

This case study is about an organization that operates in a highly competitive market with departments that produce specialized products. Each department functions with a high degree of autonomy and its department managers take pride in having primary responsibility for handling one of the most important objectives, excellent customer service before and after the sale. The company has only an OK customer satisfaction record overall, and its sales rank in the mid-range with its competitors.

Senior management felt their marginal customer service rating is related to their disappointing sales and wanted to improve the situation so they decided to move all customer service functions from each department to a new central Customer Service Department. They felt with this change, customer complaints could be handled more efficiently, boost customer satisfaction— and their sales to the next level. The new customer service department would be structured to provide direct feedback to the product designers and marketing people in a more-timely manner. Although senior management felt the changes were important, their department managers felt quite differently.

A senior manager was appointed to be the change agent and implement the restructuring. Resistance from other department managers began to grow. They complained about breaking a system that is working. Questions were raised about how centralizing customer service could work better in a company that has such a diverse product line. How could the employees there possibly understand the unique characteristics of each product and handle the array of questions that were likely to come? How could a centralized group of employees be knowledgeable enough about each product to communicate customer service issues accurately to the product's technical support people and designers? What was not voiced but was the manager's real issue was that they perceived a loss of control and status within the company, and was eventually abandoned.

Discussion

Making organizational changes is essential but can sometimes meet resistance. We often hear that people can be counted on to resist or avoid change. But, why is this avoidance to [change] so common where change is important for keeping pace with competition? The reason may not be the proposed change itself. People make changes all the time. We change where we live. We change the type of music we like and the people we dislike and then come to like. Even when unfortunate events change our lives, we usually have some choices available which gives us a feeling of having some control over the situation. Perhaps in this case the avoidance to change comes from the concern or fear of losing control, or losing standing or identity in the organization. Or because the change may threaten one's competencies.

One of the strongest elements of our human nature is the aversion to harm or to become minimized in some way. Our human nature drives us to maintain control and avoid losses. But in a workplace environment, that sense of security and control can be threatened very easily because all the options appear to be with the employer. When we feel threatened or diminished our internal alarm goes off and we react to the situation. Change agents should be willing to consider all the possible reasons if there is push back.

Fortunately, we are able to manage most of the changes we have at work reasonably well, but still even the suggestion of a change can tweak employees' responses. Here, the managers resisted the change because it reduced their perceived standing and place in the organization.

I'm not advocating plans for change should be minimized or avoided because of employees' personal concerns. The point here is to simply be aware that sometimes resistance may not be with the change itself. Take time to consider what the people involved may be feeling and talk about it openly and frankly. Show how their concerns may be unfounded, or if real, how they can be managed in some way.

We all understand businesses have a responsibility to generate sufficient income cover expenses, and change is essential for that to happen in a competitive market place. Change, is one of an organization's survival tools, but while planning for a change, it benefits change agents to address all of the realities, including their employees. One way to do this is to discuss and clarify issues to build an environment of better understanding for all.

Taking this approach may seem to be catering, pandering, or unnecessary, but the answer to this is the many facilitators who experienced unnecessary delays, derailed and unfortunate outcomes because those involved never really got on board. The change agents didn't understand something very basic; **people are as important as the process.**

Eleanor Roosevelt has been credited for saying "Happiness is not the goal; it is the by-product". I believe that simple statement is both insightful and powerful. If we translate and broaden that wisdom a bit, perhaps we can say, the *goal of change is not its success*, but being sure *all* the critical pieces of the puzzle are accounted for– because doing so provides the best chance for its by product- success. If problems do occur, they can be managed with fewer complications and with more support than would be possible otherwise.

One last point about this while referring back to those three key critical leadership traits noted Chapter Two. Leaders at any level who have those three critical leadership traits will almost always have sufficient confidence in themselves to include all of the pieces of the puzzle during the planning phase of the initiative.

I also want to mention something about the idea of being strong minded in these situations because being strong minded can be confused with being "hard headed", or difficult to work with. For the sake of this discussion, I'm using the term strong minded to describe one's ability to commit to an idea [after] there has been sufficient due diligence in fact finding, making careful assessments, and being able to see all the relevant pieces. I have worked with high-profile people who I considered to be strong minded and they were all well-liked and respected– and functioned with enough self-confidence to see all the pieces of the situation. They were also able to put [themselves] aside and learn the facts, assess information accurately, and show appropriate sensitivity– and only then be steadfast with their decision. Being strong minded does not contradict being thoughtful or not having the ability to show appropriate sensitivity for a given situation. It is being able to create the best possible conditions for change – and being able to stay the course.

Creating A Positive Environment for Change

The workplace environment needs to be suitable and able to support the change in order to have a successful outcome. The stage has to be properly set and ready. Here are a few key considerations to help prepare a workplace environment for the challenges that can come with implementing change.

- Does the organization's culture support change?
  - If the culture doesn't fit with the change, work to change the culture first or consider an alternative to the proposed change.
  - Perhaps the change can be implemented in stages as the culture adjusts
  - Make sure everyone involved understands the reason

[s] for the proposed change?

- o Determine what type of underpinning is needed to support what is being proposed. Provide proper training, new or additional equipment, etc..
- Does the plan have sufficient financial and personnel resources for making the change?
- Unlike the goat in the fable, be sure to understand the full effect of the change after implementation.
- Do the key people involved have the ability to support and implement the new procedures.
- Do what's possible to support the philosophy that people [employees] are as important as the process?

The Process

As with the other circumstances we discussed, the time needed to account for all the pieces of the puzzle often requires less time than one might imagine. Although change agents are not primarily responsible for pleasing all those who may be affected, they are accountable for doing what is possible to meet their reasonable expectations. Those expectations include things like providing updated information about how things are progressing, possible timelines, who to contact with questions, and having the reasons for a change clearly defined. And as always, it is important to maintain open two-way conversation with all who may have questions and concerns. Relevant information can be provided by assigning someone to publish project updates via email, newsletters, or depending on the situation a chat site. Doing so allows employees to get answers and also helps to prevent someone to miss interrupt, guess, or deliberately editorialize things in their favor. I have experienced situations when the change agent did not maintain good two-way communication during planning and implementation and it resulted in embarrassing trips back to the drawing board.

Here are a few other key points that can help planners increase their chance of reaching the best outcome possible.

Eight Basic Steps for Achieving A Successful Outcome for Change

- Establish convenient opportunity for on-going two-way communication.
  - o Be clear about why a change is important
    - Show how continuing without change can impact the organization standing and its employees well-being.
  - o Explain with as much clarity as possible the reality of losses and gains those involved may experience after implementation.
    - Understand perceived personal losses and do what's reasonably possible to minimize their effect.
- Define how project success will be measured.
- Summarize and make allowances for the resources that will be needed.
  - o Be sure to account for the financial, personnel, and equipment resources that are available.
- Discuss if and how other departments could be affected and be clear about any dependence there may be on other departments or services to support and comply.
- During the planning process, provide clear timelines for reaching key milestones during implementation
  - o Discuss backup plans that may be reasonable to consider
- Identify project leaders who will be available to oversee implementation.
- Be clear about the organization's commitment to making the change
  - o Be sure of the support that senior management is willing to provide
- Have a clear understanding of industry best practice and include as many of those elements as possible.

Selecting Project Managers

Choosing the [right] project manager [s] is obviously an important piece of the puzzle. There have been situations when the criteria for making this choice was based on personal relationships or an individual's political standing in the organization rather than having specific leadership competencies. So, what criteria should be used to make the best selections? The first would be to select someone who has a strong management profile and an open communication style. Chapters One and Two outline important leadership traits that should be considered.

Senior managers should be clear about which leadership traits are best suited for a given project. Complex broad scope operations require a project manager who can keep a wide range of issues in proper perspective, and of course, be able to multitask without difficulty. This individual must be able to see the forest for the trees, and the trees for the forest– and keep them in proper proportion to each other. Someone who knows how to delegate. Someone who can accurately gauge progress and be "strong minded" about making progress without getting too closely involved with the details of the process. And, someone who can be supportive and get resources from upper management if needed.

Other projects may require someone who can work more directly with those on the front line and who has a defined skill which may be needed. They must be detail oriented and able to analyze activity accurately, in a timely manner, and see how the individual pieces of the puzzle are being put in place. And, they must be able to account for all the moving pieces and keep upper management updated. Their leadership skills must be in play in order to keep everyone on the "floor" working in concert with each other. This individual must have a manner that encourages a team spirit and cooperation.

The overriding point is to not assume the obvious choice is best. One way to avoid this trap is to ask the people who he/she will be working with about the proposed leaders. Get accurate feedback about their temperament, management acumen, ability to fact find, communicate, and, of course, gain trust. Their personal integrity needs to be accounted for as well.

Evaluating the Outcome

It is essential to track progress in real-time during planning and implementation which can be accomplished by using simple tools. Planners can choose from an array of manual techniques or computer driven dashboards that are available on line to track progress. Benchmarks [way points] and their timelines should be defined during planning and monitored closely throughout implementation. The scope and complexity of a project determines the number and placement of these way points. Designate someone who is not one who is immediately involved and will have time and be available to track and provide alerts when these benchmarks are satisfied or missed.

Managing Feedback

On-site managers need to objectively evaluate feedback, including feedback that may come from employees who are working at "ground level". As "Canaries in the mine" these people are in a unique position to make worthwhile observations and give important feedback if they recognize a possible problem. It can be very tempting to ignore their message and keep the momentum of a project going, but it is wise to take a moment and check out their concerns.

Chapter Summary

> Watch for Bumps during implementation and Be Prepared to Take Corrective Action Early On
> > o Experiencing some "bumps" during implementation is a certainty no matter how perfect the plan may be. With proper planning these diversions will most likely be minor. However, if serious unforeseen and validated obstacles develop, be willing to take time for discovery and resolution.
> Be Willing to Make Adjustments on the Fly

○ Respond promptly when something indicates a problem may be at hand. Hoping problems will eventually resolve themselves can easily lead to complications and delays later. When concerns are raised someone needs to find out what is happing, why it's happening, and take corrective action if needed. In more extreme situations it may be necessary to halt implementation until the situation can be understood and worked out.

➢ Establish and Use Alliances

○ Good planning includes establishing key alliances throughout the organization with those who may be affected by the proposed change, especially since alliances can sometimes help to reinforce requests for additional resources. Financial resources need to be defined and approved as early as possible in the planning process. Sometimes changes in one department will have an unexpected impact on other departments. Consider inviting people who represent those other departments to participate in some way while planning. Here is where the lead change agent's reputation and management profile are especially important. If the project managers' profile is sufficiently high and trusted by colleagues- problems that may arise can be more easily managed or avoided all-together.

➢ Assign monitors who can accurately measure progress in real-time

○ Easy to use and interpret monitoring systems [or individuals] will be needed to track progress and untoward situations. The essential point is planners need to identify key "way points" that signal validated progress.

○ The number of way points and how finely they are calibrated will vary depending on the size and complexity of the proposed change. Each way point needs to validate key events before managers can confidently claim "mission complete" for each stage

of implementation.
> Find ways to Celebrate Milestones Reached Along the Way
  o One of the fun things about initiating change comes with opportunities to celebrate successes at all levels. In addition to having well-deserved fun, these interim celebrations help to build pride among all involved with what they are accomplishing. Doing so helps to encourage everyone's best effort.
> Maintain Strong Two-Way Communication Practices
  o Good two-way communication signals to everyone that project leaders are not taking things for granted, which in turn, gives reason for all involved to feel a part of the project and more confident.

A Final Thought

Several years ago, my boss offered a bit of advice and wisdom that proved to be useful in various circumstances over the years. As I was updating him with [perhaps too much] confidence on a major reorganization initiative, he said to remember that *the most dangerous time to ride a motorcycle is after you [think] you know how to ride it.* Implementing change in the workplace, no matter how clear the outcome may seem, should be thought of as progress only, not a with a sense of fait' a' complete'. The point is sometimes our enthusiasm encourages us to overlook subtle but important signals.

CHAPTER TEN

BEING ALERT TO THE LITTLE THINGS

The Lion and the Mouse

Once when a Lion was asleep a little Mouse began running up and down upon him; this soon wakened the Lion, who placed his huge paw upon him, and opened his big jaws to swallow him. "Pardon, O King," cried the little Mouse:

"forgive me this time, I shall never forget it: who knows but what I may be able to do you a turn some of these days?" The Lion was so tickled at the idea of the Mouse being able to help him, that he lifted up his paw and let him go. Some time after the Lion was caught in a trap, and the hunters who desired to carry him alive to the King, tied him to a tree while they went in search of a waggon to carry him on. Just then the little Mouse happened to pass by, and seeing the sad plight in which the Lion was, went up to him and soon gnawed away the ropes that bound the King of the Beasts. "Was I not right?" said the little Mouse.

Little friends may prove great friends

Conclusion and Practical Application

Know when to lead and when to follow—*Listen and Heed the message*— as subtle or unlikely as it may be.

Case Study

Mary had been managing her department of approximately two hundred employees for more than ten years, and is one of several departments that work together within a large division. Alison had been recently hired to manage the division. Mary's department was relatively efficient, but had high employee turnover and filling vacancies was surprisingly difficult despite the large pool of qualified talent that was available in the surrounding communities. Employee complaints were low except for random issues that seemed to be resolved without difficulty. All the managers in Alison's division worked well together and Alison began to rely on Mary's long tenure in the division to learn about its history and also began to see Mary as a very competent manager.

Alison began the practice of making rounds occasionally and walked through her departments to say hello to employees and observe operations firsthand. These were casual visits, often not being more than five or ten minutes in each department. Conversations with employees and supervisors on these occasions ranged from how the day was going to comments about operations in general. However, after a number of these visits to Mary's department, Alison became increasingly aware that something was missing with the responses she got from employees. They were different from conversations she had with employees in other departments. Here, the responses were friendly but truncated, and after a while Alison had a clear sense that something wasn't as it should be. Alison would occasionally take the opportunity to sit in during her manger's department staff meetings and found the meetings Mary had with her employees also felt different. There was less free conversation and it was mostly one-way, from Mary. Also, there was virtually no questions from employees about problems that had been discussed during previous meetings.

After a few months of these observations, Alison mentioned this to Mary who became surprisingly casual. With Alison's growing feeling that something more may be happening, she asked how Mary felt about scheduling an open discussion with her employees to talk about ideas and ways they could possibly improve operations or make their work easier. Mary didn't object, but was not enthusiastic about the idea. The meeting was scheduled and had only moderate attendance. Some issues where discussed, but nothing appeared to be of major concern. Satisfied with the outcome, Alison felt better but shortly after, one of Mary's employees asked Alison's secretary for time to meet with Alison.

The employee was reluctant at first, but after getting an assurance of confidentiality, she explained her feelings to Alison about the work environment. She described Mary as a competent manager but one whose decisions were unpredictable and at times seemed to be arbitrary. Further, she indicated it was not unusual for Mary to respond harshly to an employee in a manner that verged on being abusive. She said working in this environment made employees feel uneasy and sometimes feared for their jobs, especially if Mary felt challenged. This feedback raised concerns again and also created a problem for Alison. On one hand she had come to trust and rely on Mary's advice, but Alison didn't feel she could ignore what may be a problem with Mary's management style. Alison knew she needed to be careful but she didn't want to ignore the employee's expressed concerns.

Alison took everything she knew at the time into account and had to decide whether to listen to the "mouse in the room" or trust Mary and take no action. Alison asked Mary if she would schedule a meeting with the employees in her absence. Mary was resistant but agreed. At the meeting, a few employees who Alison recognized from her walk-throughs as being fair minded gave specific examples of their concerns. Alison came to the conclusion that her uncertainty had grounding and are supported by specific examples.

Alison talked with Mary about this afterward and asked Mary to give her management style some thought and consider taking a slightly different approach when working with her employees. A week later, Mary met with Alison to have a follow up discussion and two things became immediately evident. First, Mary had taken a decidedly defensive approach while minimizing her employee's feelings and second, she was clearly driven by a philosophy that showing flexibility and being "too soft" with her employees shows weakness. A weakness that Mary believed her employees could take advantage of and lead to a loss of control.

A short while after this meeting an unsettling incident occurred with Mary and an employee. Alison talked with Mary again about her approach but felt after hearing Mary's explanation she was at least trying something different. However, not long after another troublesome personnel situation came to light that could not be justified or overlooked.

Alison considered Mary's long-term employment and continued to counsel Mary without seeing improvement. Several weeks later, two of Mary's employees talked with Alison about an incident which indicated Mary's approach had not changed at all, and Alison decided to talk with an HR representative. The HR person told Alison they had received employee complaints in the past as well and agreed it was time for a change. Alison asked for Mary's resignation. During the following weeks, Alison's actions appeared to be very much on track as additional anecdotes surfaced about how Mary exercised her authority and sometimes threatened her employees in various ways.

Discussion

In situations like these, it's critically important for the senior manager to maintain a balanced position when employees report problems regarding their boss. These "small" voices as we see in the fable can provide Information and help that shouldn't be ignored, but they also need to be calculated carefully and properly balanced and measured with reality. It's certainly not unusual for employees to complain about their boss's actions or inactions, but sometimes these concerns do carry a slightly different feel and need be followed up with discretion.

To help establish this balance, the senior manager needs to <u>take time</u> to fact – find and not be rushed in anyway. What confused Alison initially was that Mary had held her position for many years without any apparent difficulties. In this situation, Mary's employees liked their jobs, and their coworkers despite their workplace conditions, and decided to work together under the circumstances in the best possible way. They learned to develop techniques and strategies they felt made the situation manageable. However, doing this created other problems for themselves and their work. They began to spend too much time thinking about how to stay out of trouble and manage their environment instead of how they could do a better job or provide better customer service. They learned to accept their workplace as it was and had little additional energy and willingness to solve problems or suggest improvements.

Clearly, scheduling a meeting with employees without their supervisor or manager attending requires a great deal of sensitivity and caution, and could be done by an outside facilitator. But in either case, it first must be discussed with the manager in advance with clearly defined reasons, and with the objective of finding ways that could benefit all those who are involved. If there are issues that can be validated in the workplace, the manager or supervisor are probably feeling stress as well and doing something that can relieve their stress would certainly be worth the effort. The objective here was to find ways to support the manager by discussing the issues in a none threatening supportive way and providing time and opportunities to improve.

Sometimes an outside facilitator can help with this, but Alison felt confident she could manage and maintain proper focus. She was a known quantity to Mary's employees by this time because of her rounding. She knew she had to depersonalize the situation and focus on the affect of what was happening, not the person. She felt she could accomplish this by focusing on what could be done to benefit all who were involved to the extent possible rather than assign blame. Also, in almost all of these situations it is rarely only one piece of an operation that is causing the problem [s]. In this case Mary's actions may well be triggered by other circumstances and if so, those contributing issues needs to be resolved. The best approach for accomplishing this is to get all of the issues on the table with open and respectful discussion that focuses only on the facts.

■ Chapter Summary

- ➤ Senior leaders should be open and willing to follow up on concerns regarding a managers' conduct, style, or management philosophy.
    - ○ Sometimes that little voice we hear inside has validity
    - ○ Be careful to not under or overestimate a seemingly casual comment.
    - ○ Ask questions discretely, get more than one point of view regarding the concern.
    - ○ If validated, proceed in a more direct manner to understand the details.
- ➤ If the issues are sufficiently defined and validated, talk with the manager.
    - ○ Get the manager's feedback in order to clarify the circumstances
    - ○ Consider other extenuating circumstances that may be influencing the manager's conduct or approach.
- ➤ If concerns can be validated
    - ○ Discuss opportunities for making improvements
    - ○ Provide support with coaching and provide opportunities for formal training.
    - ○ This is a time for support and encouragement not accusations
- ➤ Depending on the nature of the problem, consider getting assistance from HR
- ➤ Move to counselling if sufficient progress is not made
    - ○ Document progress in sufficient detail and in a timely manner.
    - ○ Define an action plan with the person and establish timelines to see improvement
    - ○ Be clear about what needs to be improved
- ➤ Track the individual's progress
- ➤ If progress is not acceptable, continue with a higher level of disciplinary action.

Wrapping It Up

The Oxen and the Lion

- <u>Team Building:</u> Leaders are responsible for providing a clear vision of philosophy, purpose, and practice together with clearly defined performance expectations. Team leaders need to provide support through coaching, mentoring, and by example, and provide a safe environment for discussion and disagreement.

The Mule and the Purchaser

- <u>Management Competency and Hiring Criteria:</u> A central and essential responsibility of leadership is to assess competencies of managers and provide opportunities to develop those skills and competencies. Operations become more efficient and employee morale is strengthened when managers satisfy the two Dimensions of Management. Using the three key management traits [intellect, wisdom, and commonsense] are essential to providing strong and effective leadership at all levels.

The Man, the Boy, and the Donkey

- <u>Resolving Employee Conflicts</u>: Effective and timely decisions can be made by defining clear boundaries for making decisions and being open to employees' suggestions for solutions. The primary objective is to support the organization's objectives while considering the employees' reasonable concerns. Weighting decisions to heavily on an employee or group's of employees interests will lead to disfunction.

The Eagle and the Arrow

- <u>Verbal Communication</u>: Is a practiced skill, not a science. When speaking we have the responsibility to create a communication package that clearly defines the message and is in balance with the circumstances. The responsibility of those listening is to stay focused to what is being said without over or under interpreting the message. Be willing to ask questions to get clarification. Show courtesy by providing opportunity for additional discussion.

The Boy and the Filberts

- <u>Trying to Solve Too Many Problems at the Same Time</u> Attempting to solve multiple management problems at the same time can be overwhelming and will complicate the situation by making pre-mature decisions. The initial step is to follow a regimen to fact find each situation, determine the sequence for implementing action plans.

The Mountains in Labour

- <u>Finding Resolution to Long Standing Operations Problems:</u> Having meetings about operations problems is not-taking action. Avoid meetings when valuable time is waisted with repeated anecdotes or explanations that are intended to deflect accountability. Focus on root cause and demand compliance to specific performance standards.

The Young Thief and His Mother

- <u>Meeting Performance Standards:</u> Defaulting to counselling or discipline when errors occur is often a less productive strategy. Be careful the match the training to the details of the task. Ongoing training encourages all employees to function at their highest level of proficiency and accuracy. Be open to creative training methods. Training programs increase the value of each employee.

Belling the Cat

- <u>Great Sounding Solutions:</u> Even the best sounding solutions need to be researched and have proper underpinning. The enthusiasm that comes with moving ahead on a great idea can cause other problems if full disclosure of the circumstances is not achieved. Question the contingencies and assumptions an action plan is based upon.

The Fox and the Goat

- <u>Look Carefully Before You Leap</u>: One should first make careful and objective assessments of the need for change. Be clear about the objectives, overall value, and feasibility of implementation. Make sure all the stake holders and those who will be impacted by the change have appropriate opportunity to weigh in. Remember, people are as important as the process.

The Lion and the Mouse

- <u>Observe Subtleties</u>: Be careful to give appropriate weight to random or subtle comments about management personnel or workplace situations. A casual follow-up assessment is the first step. Take reasonable and appropriate steps to investigate while remembering the essential responsibility a leader has to his/ her managers is to provide support and guidance.

www.ingramcontent.com/pod-product-compliance
Lightning Source LLC
Chambersburg PA
CBHW031437120626
46545CB00006B/2442